FENCE
—the—
FRAUD

A Practical Guide to Prevent Bank Frauds
(Cheque and Card)

FENCE the FRAUD

A Practical Guide to Prevent Bank Frauds
(Cheque and Card)

KANWAR MEHTA

Notion Press

Old No. 38, New No. 6
McNichols Road, Chetpet
Chennai - 600 031

First Published by Notion Press 2016
Copyright © Kanwar Mehta 2016
All Rights Reserved.

ISBN 978-1-945825-13-2

This book has been published with all efforts taken to make the material error-free after the consent of the author. However, the author and the publisher do not assume and hereby disclaim any liability to any party for any loss, damage, or disruption caused by errors or omissions, whether such errors or omissions result from negligence, accident, or any other cause.

No part of this book may be used, reproduced in any manner whatsoever without written permission from the author, except in the case of brief quotations embodied in critical articles and reviews.

I dedicate this book, with respect and love to my parents.

CONTENTS

About the Author — xi
Preface — xiii
Acknowledgements — xv
Introduction — xvii

SECTION 1   CHEQUE FRAUDS

1. Cheque — 3
2. Various Types of Other Cheques — 4
3. Parties to Cheque — 5
   a. Drawer — 5
   b. The payee — 5
   c. Drawee — 6
4. Cheque Payment — 6
   a. Bearer Cheque — 7
   b. Order Cheque — 7
   c. Crossed Cheque — 8
5. Category of Cheques — 9
   a. Cash Cheque — 9
   b. Transfer Cheque — 9
   c. Clearing Cheque — 9
   d. Outstation Cheque — 10
   e. Local Cheque — 10
   f. At Par Cheque — 10
   g. Post Dated Cheque — 10
   h. Mutilated Cheque — 10
   i. Stale Cheque — 11
   j. Return/Bounced/Dishonoured Cheque — 11
6. Stop Payment of a Cheque — 11
7. Validity of the Cheque — 12

Contents

8.	Type of Crossing of Cheques	12
	a. Cheque crossed generally	12
	b. Cheque crossed specially	13
	c. A/C Payee only	13
9.	Endorsement of Cheques	13
10.	Endorsement of Cheques by Banks	14
11.	Other Significant Terms/Information	14
	a. Role of Clearing House	14
	b. Magnetic Ink Character Recognition (MICR)	15
	c. Cheque Truncation System (CTS)	18
	d. Indian Financial Code System (IFSC)	18
12.	Other Payment Systems	19
	a. Electronic Clearing Service (ECS)	19
	b. National Electronic Fund Transfer (NEFT)	19
	c. Real Time Gross Settlement (RTGS)	20
	d. Immediate Payment Service (IMPS)	20
	e. Mobile Wallet	20
13.	Cheque Frauds	20
14.	Type of Cheque Frauds	22
	a. Counterfeit Cheques	22
	b. Stolen Cheques	23
	c. Altered Cheques	23
	d. Forged Cheques (signature)	24
	e. Forged Cheques (endorsement)	24
	f. Cheques drawn on a closed account	24
	g. Cheques drawn as to look like Demand Draft or Banker Cheque	24
15.	Case events of Cheque Frauds	24
16.	How to avoid Cheque Frauds	39
17.	Safety of Cheque Book	39
	a. Verify and count all the cheque leaves	40
	b. Keep the cheque book in a safe place	40
	c. Follow your cheque book when in transit	40
	d. Record of cheques issued	41
	e. Stop Payment of unused Cheques	41
	f. Safe Custody of Cheque Book	41
18.	Cheque Requisition Slip	41

Contents

19.	Writing the Cheque	42
20.	Other Precautions	44
21.	Precautionary Tips on Receiving and Accepting Cheques/Bankers Cheques/Drafts from others	45
22.	Precautionary Tips for Bank Staff handling Cheque Transactions	47
	a. Inward Clearing Cheques (Paying Bank)	49
	b. Outward Clearing Cheques (Presenting Bank)	51

SECTION 2 ATM/DEBIT/CREDIT CARD FRAUDS

1.	The Need and importance of Cards (ATM/Debit/Credit Cards)	55
2.	Classification of Cards	56
	a. ATM/Debit Cards	56
	b. Credit Cards	56
	c. Prepaid Cards	56
3.	Other Important Information about Cards	57
	a. Visa/Master Card/Maestro	57
	b. RuPay Cards	57
	c. International usages of Cards	57
	d. Personal Identification Number (PIN)	57
	e. One Time Password (OTP)	58
	f. Credit Verification Value (CVV)	58
4.	How to use Cards	58
5.	Automated Teller Machine (ATM)	59
6.	White Label ATM (WLA)	59
7.	Location wise Classification of Automated Teller Machine (ATM)	60
8.	Type of Cards used at an ATM	60
9.	Advantage of ATMs	61
10.	Banks Advantages	61
11.	Customers Advantages	61
12.	Comparison of ATM Card with a Debit Card and a Credit Card	62
13.	How to Operate Automated Teller Machine (ATM)?	63
14.	Stepwise process of operating the ATM	64

15.	Failed Transactions-Account debited cash not disbursed	66
16.	What to do in case your card is Stuck in ATM	66
17.	ATM operational Complaints	66
18.	Card Frauds-ATM Frauds	67
19.	Type of ATM frauds	68
	a. Card Theft	68
	b. Personal Identification Number (PIN) Stealing	69
	c. Card Skimming	69
20.	Important Tips to safeguard from ATM/Debit/Credit Card Frauds	70
21.	Safety and Security tips while using Cards at ATM	73
	a. Pre-processing Situations	73
	b. Processing and Post Processing Situation	74
22.	Point of Sale (POS) System	76
23.	Process of use of debit/credit card for retail transactions at Point of sale terminal	77
24.	Safety Tips-Uses of Debit/Credit Cards at Merchant Establishments	77
25.	Victim of Card frauds-Some case studies	78

SECTION 3   MANAGEMENT OF BANK FRAUDS-CHEQUE AND CARD

1.	Management of Bank Frauds	87
2.	What to do in case of Cheque Frauds	88
3.	What to do in case of other type of Cheque Frauds	91
4.	What to do in case of Card (ATM/Debit/Credit Card) Frauds	91
	a. Card switched with Fake Card (Card Stolen)	92
	b. ATM card with the cardholder but money withdrawn from an ATM	92
5.	Other forum for immediate relief for Bank Customers	94
	a. Banking Ombudsman Scheme	94
	b. Consumer Forum	96
6.	Fraud Cases Settled by Banking Ombudsman	98
	a. Cheque Fraud Cases	98
	b. Card fraud cases	100
7.	Conclusion	102

ABOUT THE AUTHOR

Mr. Kanwar Mehta has been a banker par excellence in a career spanning more than 30 years. He has worked with premier nationalized and private sector banks performing various roles and most importantly in a mix of customer facing and complex operational environment. After contributing for more than 2 decades to Vijaya Bank, Mr. Kanwar Mehta worked with Bank of Punjab, Centurion Bank, Centurion Bank of Punjab and HDFC Bank in the latter part of his career.

He was a successful and popular banker and worked in various capacities namely, Branch Head, Head Operations. -Foreign Exchange Services and Head Fraud Investigation Cell. While he is credited with re-designing key operational processes around Foreign Exchange Services and Money Transfer, he was instrumental in training staff at the banks he worked with on various banking topics and specifically on prevention of bank frauds.

He received a number of merit certificates as his branches were declared outstanding during regular performance reviews. A good team leader he was known to keep his co-workers inculcating a culture of high achievement and excellence.

About the Author

He has investigated and solved number of bank fraud cases and has helped both banks and customers in fighting the growing menace of frauds. Post his last role at HDFC Bank, Mr. Mehta got attached to the mission of helping and educating customers of banks and financial services organizations, who become victims of bank frauds, in mitigating or recovering losses. He is also passionate about sharing knowledge and educating people on prevention of frauds. The knowledge and understanding of cases that he worked on gave him the thrust to start his own venture, "Complete Trust Solutions", a consultancy service to help and advice those who become victims of bank frauds.

His experience of working with Delhi Police and Central Bureau of Investigation (CBI) for more than six years before joining the banking sector gives him critical insights and an intuitive mind set when approaching matters related to fraud, embezzlement and cheating where innocent and unsuspecting public is targeted.

His goal that he strives to achieve with utmost passion is to help people get justice, provide them the guidance to recover their money lost due to fraud and educate them to prevent such instances.

This book "Fence the Fraud" is another step to reach out to people and bankers to achieve his goal. For more of Kanwar Mehta's ideas or services related to consultation, workshops and training contact him through web site www.completetrust.in.

PREFACE

Cheques and Cards (ATM/Debit/Credit) are very important payment instruments. We use them frequently for cash withdrawal from our bank account and for a number of other financial transactions such as transfer of funds from one account to another, third party payments, etc. Credit and Debit cards are also used for authorization of online transactions and for purchase of goods and services.

These instruments are quite vulnerable to fraud. Recently, we have seen a spike in the number of frauds reported by the media. This has become a big challenge not only for all of us, but also for business institutions, Banks, Reserve Bank of India, Police and other agencies.

I came across a number of cheques and card frauds while working for more than 30 years with different Banks. I also got an opportunity to work as Head Fraud Investigating Cell of a Bank and investigated and solved a number of such frauds. I also got the opportunity to speak to some of the fraudsters/culprits and was able to understand their motives behind the act.

As per psychologists there are three elements, motivation (need for money), opportunity and rationalization, present in every fraud. This is true because I have observed that a number of frauds occur as we give these fraudsters the opportunity to commit fraud. So we have to be very careful while doing our financial transactions and never provide any opportunity to culprits to take our money.

It is a matter of concern that most of the customers of a bank get to know about the cheque frauds or ATM/Debit/Credit card frauds only when they become victims of such frauds.

Post my retirement I thought I should write a book on cheques and card frauds and share my experience with the common man so that they can benefit and learn to prevent the same. In fact, we need to learn the basic tips and if we apply the same in handling our banking transactions I am sure that nobody can cheat us.

I have used very simple language so that everyone can understand all about cheques and card frauds.

I intend to share my knowledge and experience through this book and ensure that everyone understands about cheque and card frauds. This book is also aimed at being useful for beginning a career in banking as well as serve bankers so that they can learn to handle cheques as well as the matters relating to card transactions.

I hope the readers will benefit greatly from this book and save their hard earned money.

Kanwar Mehta

ACKNOWLEDGEMENTS

This book is a culmination of the vision, patience and understanding of my wife Dr. Karuna Mehta who encouraged me to pen down my experiences.

I appreciate the support of my sons Madhur Mehta and Aakash Mehta who devoted time to go through the manuscript and made valuable suggestions.

I express my heartfelt gratitude to my loving grandson Viraj Mehta for keeping me active, energetic and in good humour because of which I could write this book.

I am grateful to all for their wishes and blessings.

INTRODUCTION

Banks all over the world are facing a big challenge of providing safe banking to their customers and constantly putting all their efforts in the same. However, one class of criminals is always working to counter the efforts of the banks putting more pressure on them. The history of Bank frauds is as old as the history of any activity started by banks related to monetary transactions.

Cheques and Cards (Credit Card/ATM Cards/Debit Cards) are two very important instruments used for our financial transactions.

The origin of the cheque can be traced to the seventeenth century, whereas the origin of cards came later in the mid-nineties.

In India the first credit card was introduced in 1980 by the Central Bank. The transactions of ATM card started with the introduction of first Automated Teller Machine (ATM) in the year 1967 in United Kingdom. In India the first Automated Teller Machine (ATM) was introduced in the year 1987 by HSBC bank and thereafter other banks also introduced ATMs and by March 2007 the total numbers of ATMs stood at around 27000. Currently, more than 180000 ATMs have been installed.

Introduction

First Debit Card came into existence in the year 1966. In India the first Debit Card was issued by Citibank in the year 1987.

The intention to introduce Automated Teller Machines (ATMs) was to improve customer service by providing round the clock 24/7 cash withdrawal facility to Bank customers through these machines installed at various locations.

Nowadays when another avenue for payment, such as Online Banking and Credit Card are available still the ATM/Debit cards are widely used for the withdrawal of cash and other activities. The usages of cheques for self-withdrawal of cash has been reduced, but still the same are used for third party payments.

The Banks are very serious about all types of frauds taking place in banks and have taken a number of preventive steps to stop them, but in spite of this the fraudsters are successfully able to take out the hard earned money from the accounts of the customers of the banks.

Another main reason for Cheque and Card frauds is that fraudsters, nowadays, have very easy access to low cost technology like professional desktop publishing and copying technology, colour copiers, laser printers, scanners which they use to make fraudulent instruments and documents.

The increase in the number of Cheques and Cards frauds is of a serious concern for the Reserve Bank of India, Police Department, all banks and its clients. The need of the hour is to do something more to avoid the same.

INTRODUCTION

This book is an effort to educate the customers of banks, general public, bank staff and the victims of cheques and card frauds about various types of cheque and Card frauds and the preventive steps need to be taken to avoid the same. What are the remedies available in case of fraudulent transaction in the bank account are also covered in this book. The book is divided into three sections. The first section covers Cheque Frauds. The second covers the Card Frauds. The third section covers the actions to be taken by the victims of cheque and card frauds.

A careful reading of my book will help the reader understand the type of cheques frauds and card frauds taking place and how best the same can be prevented.

Section 1

CHEQUE FRAUDS

1. Cheque

To understand about cheque frauds it is very important to first know all about a Cheque and the process of cheque payments. A very simple way to understand all about cheques is given in this chapter.

As per Article 6 of the Negotiable Instruments Act, 1881 as amended from time to time "A cheque is a bill of exchange drawn on a specified banker and not expressed to be payable otherwise than on demand and it includes the electronic image of a truncated cheque and a cheque in electronic form."

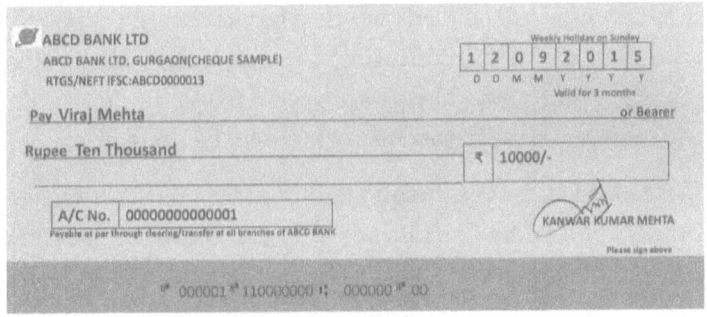

Normal Cheque

Cheque is a very important instrument provided by a bank to its customers, individuals/firms/companies, on the opening of their saving bank account, current account or any other type of running account such as cash credit and overdraft loan. The cheques are provided with a cheque book which contain 10/25/100 cheque leaves. Each cheque has running serial number. Bank customers write these cheques to operate their account by filling the date, name of the payee/beneficiary and amount in figure and words. The cheque is also signed by the customer before giving it to the beneficiary. The account holder also uses the cheques for cash withdrawal. The cheque book also contains cheque requisition slip which is used by the customer to request for a new cheque book. The cheque book also contains record sheets for recording the cheque transactions.

2. Various Types of Other Cheques

Various other types of below mentioned Cheques are also issued by the banks. The main difference between cheques and these instruments is that the same are prepaid instruments and issued by the Banks for the specific amount only after collecting the full value plus some charges, whereas the cheques are provided to the customers for issuing the same toward their financial obligations.

Demand Draft- Is a cheque that contains an order of one branch of the bank (Drawer Branch) directing another branch of the same bank (Drawee branch) to pay on demand a certain sum of money to specified beneficiaries (Payee). Mainly issued at the request of the customers on outstation branches for commercial payment.

Pay Order/Banker Cheque/Cashier Cheque- Payable on the issuing branch of the bank. Mainly issued by the banks for local commercial payments.

Gift Cheque-A cheque used for gifting money on various occasions instead of hard cash.

Traveller Cheque- A cheque for a fixed amount that may be cashed or used in payment abroad and in practice at most hotels, shops etc. after endorsement by the holder's signature.

3. PARTIES TO CHEQUE

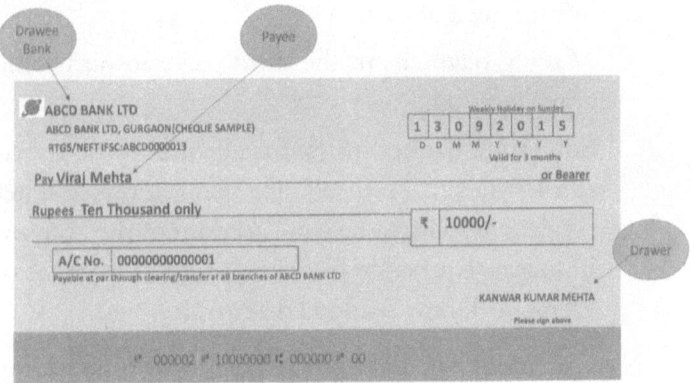

a. Drawer

The person who sign the Cheque.

b. The payee

A person who is due to be paid; e.g. a cheque is made payable to a payee and he is entitled to cash it.

c. Drawee

The Bank to whom the cheque is drawn.

4. Cheque Payment

Cheque Payment is one of very important functions of the bank. When any person opens his account in a Bank and deposit money in the account a cheque book containing 10/25/100 cheque leaves is provided to the account holder to operate the account. The cheque payment process starts when the account holder issues the cheques for the following purpose:

   a. Withdrawal of cash.
   b. Making payment to the third party toward some consideration.
   c. Sometime banker insists for cheques to be issued in their favour (Yourself) for the purpose of other services for which the bank account of the account holder is required to be debited such as issuance of Demand Draft, Banker Cheque etc.

Now, as mentioned above the person who issues the cheque is called "Drawer" and the one who receives the cheque issued in his favour is called "Payee" and the bank on whom the cheque is issued is called "Drawee" bank. To get the payment of the cheques the payee needs to go either to the Drawee bank, if he is having an account in the same bank, or to his banker where he is maintaining his account.

The customer also needs to know the details of different type of cheques, as given below, available with the banks, which entitled the payee to get the payment from the paying bank on presentation:

a. Bearer Cheque

The cheque is drawn in favour of the payee who is entitled to encash the same. However, when the cheque is payable to the payee or bearer and the drawer is not cancelling the bearer, the cheque become the bearer Cheque.

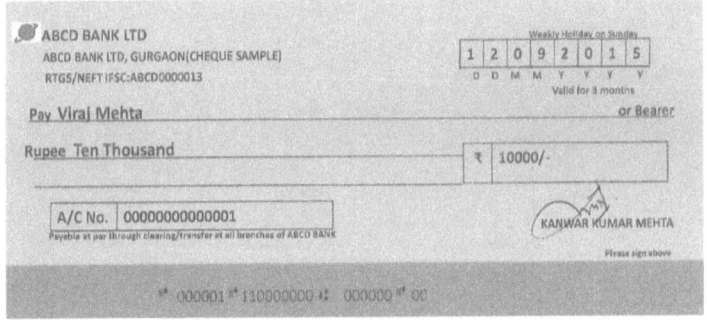

Bearer Cheque

Such cheques can be paid at the counter of paying bank to the presenter of the cheque.

b. Order Cheque

Banks mostly provide cheques to the customer having "Or Bearer" printed on it. However, cheques printed "Or Order" are also being provided or when customer cancels 'Bearer' and writes 'Order' then the cheque become payable to the payee.

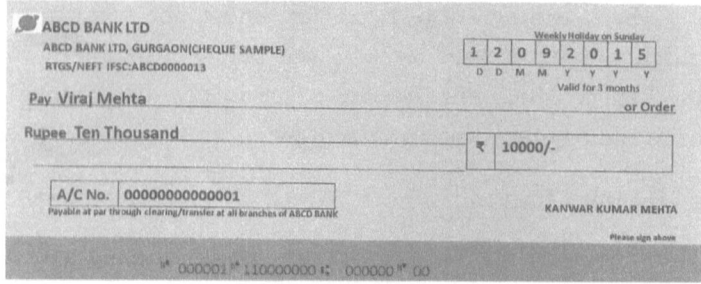

Order Cheque

- The payee, however, can transfer the cheque by endorsement.

c. Crossed Cheque

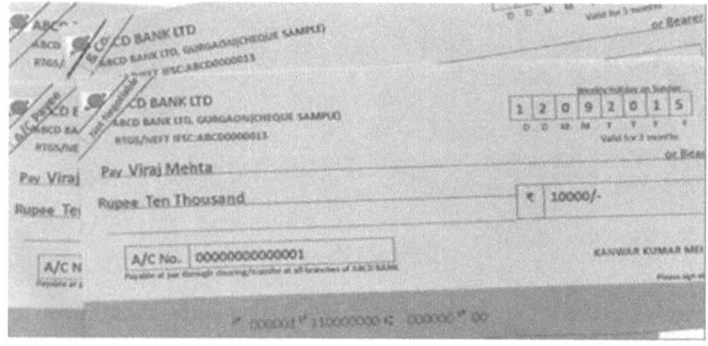

Crossed Cheques

The cheque crossed by drawing two parallel lines on the top left corner with or without additional words is called crossed cheque.

Crossed Cheque is paid by banks by crediting the account of the payee.

5. Category of Cheques

The banks mainly categorize cheques into the following categories on the basis of their functionality while handling or making the payment. These cheques are presented by their account holders either drawn on them or on other banks:

a. Cash Cheque

Payment made by the drawee bank in cash against the cheque either to the customer of the bank or to third party who presented the cheque to the drawee bank on their counter to get cash payment is mainly categorized as Cash Cheque. In a simple terms all the cheques paid in cash by the banks are known as cash cheques. These cheques are debited to the customer's account.

b. Transfer Cheque

Payment transferred from one account to the other account in the same bank in respect of a cheque deposited by the payee is categorized as Transfer Cheque. In such cases the drawer and the payee maintain account in the same bank.

c. Clearing Cheque

The payment of a cheque drawn on other bank is collected through Clearing. This types of cheque is categorised as Clearing Cheque in most of the banks. In such cases the payee maintains accounts in Bank A and receive a Cheque issued in his favour drawn on Bank B. Bank A collects the payment on behalf of its customer from Bank B through a clearing house.

d. Outstation Cheque

The Cheque drawn and payable at cities other than the city where the payee is having his bank account is known as outstation cheque. The proceeds of the outstation cheque is collected by the payee's bank by sending the same to the drawee bank through its own branch or to the branch of other bank. However it is very important to note that the proceeds of at par cheque can be collected from any of the local branch of the drawee bank.

e. Local Cheque

Cheques drawn and payable at the same city are categorised as local cheques. The paying bank can collect the proceeds of the local cheque by presenting the same in the local clearing. At par cheques can also be categorised as Local cheque.

f. At Par Cheque

Cheque payable at all the branches of the Drawee bank. The banks issue cheque book printed on each cheque leaf "Payable at all our branches in India."

g. Post Dated Cheque

Cheque issued by the drawer in favour of the payee on a future date is known as post-dated cheque. The payment of the cheque however can be collected on the date of the cheque.

h. Mutilated Cheque

Cheque in torn condition is called mutilated cheque. The payment of such cheques can be collected only if the presenting banks take the responsibility by way of an endorsement on the back side of the mutilated cheque. The payment of such cheque can also be made after getting the confirmation of the drawer.

i. Stale Cheque

The validity of Cheques/Pay orders/Drafts/Banker Cheques is 3 months from the date they have been drawn. The cheque presented after the expiry of three month is called the stale cheque.

j. Return/Bounced/Dishonoured Cheque

Cheque that cannot be paid by banks on presentation on their counters by payee either through clearing or in person are returned to the presenter. These cheques are known as Return/Bounced/Dishonoured Cheques. Cheques are returned unpaid due to insufficient funds in the drawers account or due to other reasons, such as alteration on the cheque, payment stopped by the drawer, post-dated cheque, stale cheque etc.

6. STOP PAYMENT OF A CHEQUE

The drawer of a cheque can stop payment of a cheque already issued and delivered to the beneficiary. The bank will accept such stop payment instructions against acknowledgement and note the stop payment of the same in their records provided the cheque has not already been paid. The charges for noting the stop payment is recovered by the bank from the account of the drawer of the cheque.

Nowadays bank customers can also stop the payment of the cheque themselves, round the clock, through internet banking.

7. Validity of the Cheque

Presently, the validity of the Cheque/Pay orders/Drafts/Banker Cheques is 3 months from the date they have been drawn. Traveller Cheque is valid for unlimited period.

8. Type of Crossing of Cheques

The cheque are generally issued either for the withdrawal of cash from the account or for making payment to the third party. In case of withdrawal of cash by self, the cheque is being issued to "Self". The payment of cheque issued to self can be collected by the third Party also provided the cheque is issued as "Pay Self / Mr. ABC or Bearer.

When the payment is to be made to a third party, the cheque is generally crossed by putting two parallel transverse lines on the left side corner of the cheque with or without words. This is to ensure that the payment of the cheque is received by the right person. It also ensures that the payment is to be made in the account of the payee. The above action is known as crossing of cheques and has been legally defined under the Negotiable Instrument Act, 1881.

The following two types of crossing of cheques have been defined in the Negotiable act:

a. Cheque crossed generally

Where a cheque bears across its face an addition of the words "and company" or any abbreviation thereof, between two parallel transverse lines or of two parallel transverse lines simply, either with or without the words "not negotiable", that addition shall be deemed a crossing, and the cheque shall be deemed to be crossed generally. The payment of such cheque can be collected by any bank where the payee is maintaining his account.

b. Cheque crossed specially

Where cheques bear across its face an addition of the name of the banker, either with or without the words "not negotiable", that addition shall be deemed a crossing or the cheque shall be deemed to be crossed specially, and to be crossed to that banker. The payment of such cheques can be collected by the banker whose name is added across the face of the cheque.

c. A/C Payee only

One more crossing "A/C Payee only" is also very much used, whereas the Negotiable Instruments Act is silent about this type of crossing. In practice the proceeds of a cheque having this crossing is credited to the bank account of the payee only and also cannot be endorsed in favour of any third party.

9. ENDORSEMENT OF CHEQUES

As per Negotiable Instruments Act, 1881 when the maker or the holder of a negotiable instrument signs the same on the back, he is said to have endorsed the same, and is called the "endorser". When endorser signs his name only, the endorsement is said to be "in blank", and if he adds a direction to pay the amount mentioned in the instrument to, or the order of, a specified person, the endorsement is said to be "in full" and the person so specified is called the "endorsee" of the instrument. The Cheque issued with crossing can be endorsed in favour of a third party by the payee.

10. Endorsement of Cheques by Banks

Cheques and other instruments received from customers drawn on different banks are to be endorsed appropriately by the collecting bank before its presentation to the drawee bank.

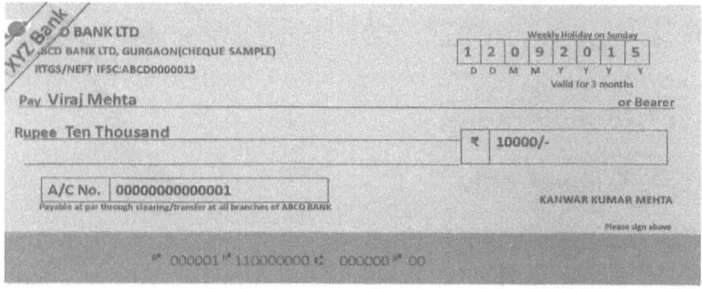

Such cheques on receipt from the customers should be affixed with special crossing stamps (the name of the bank and branch to be incorporated in two parallel lines) as shown above.

11. Other Significant Terms/Information

a. Role of Clearing House

As given in the Negotiable Instruments Act, 1881 the expression "clearing house" means the clearing house managed by the Reserve Bank of India or a clearing house recognized as such by the Reserve Bank of India.

In a simple way to understand the role of the Clearing House is that it provides a platform to all the banks to exchange cheques drawn on other banks, deposited by their customers on their counters. So when banks receive cheques drawn on various other banks from their customers they exchange these cheques through the clearing house. So each bank receives all cheques drawn on them and delivers all other cheques drawn on other banks. The difference of the total amount of the cheques received and delivered is credited/debited to the respective bank account maintained with the clearing house.

In respect of the cheques which the drawee/paying bank return for any reasons are exchanged in return clearing and the difference of the amount is credited/debited to the respective bank account.

The process of exchange of cheques in clearing house is known as **Inward Clearing** and **Outward Clearing**. Cheques received by a bank from other banks are known as Inward Clearing and cheques drawn on other banks and presented to them is known as Outward Clearing. All banks simultaneously handle both the inward and outward clearings.

b. Magnetic Ink Character Recognition (MICR)

Codes appears at the bottom of the cheque, printed in magnetic ink, that can be read by the machines are known as MICR codes. This process brought a revolution in to the banking industry when the same was introduced in the year 1980. It made the clearing of cheques very easy and fast.

The numbers at the bottom (MICR band) represent the following:

First Set (000002) Represents Cheque Number.

Second Set (110000000) represents MICR Code. First three (000) Represent City Code. Second three (000) Represent Bank Code. Last three (000) Represent Branch Code.

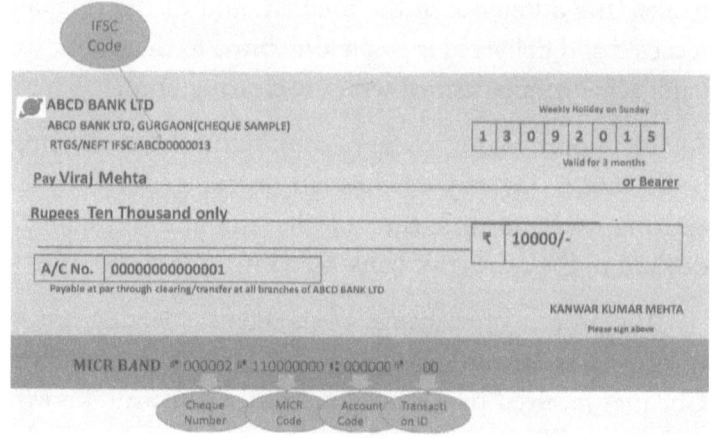

MICR Cheque

Third Set (000000) Code Represents Account number field, consisting of six digits followed by a delimiter, is an optional field. In the case of Government Cheques issued by RBI alone, the account number is of seven digits. The Government Account number is 10 digits in length – 7 digits occurring in the Account number field and three in the transaction code field.

Fourth Set (00) Code Represents transaction ID. This is a uniform set of transaction codes used by all the banks.

The transaction code, to be pre-printed, comprises a two digit number running from 1 to 99. Codes 01 to 49 are reserved for debit instruments and codes 50 to 99 for credit instruments.

After migration to Cheque Truncation System (CTS), the traditional MICR-based cheque processing has been discontinued across the country. The MICR codes are still relevant and continued to be appeared on the cheques as the same are used to identify a bank-branch and other relevant information.

The following id codes are relevant to cheque transactions and are printed on the cheques as shown above:

Code Nature of Transaction

10 Savings Bank Account Cheques (Local use)

11 Current Account Cheques (Local use)

12 Banker's Cheques

13 Cash Credit A/C Cheques (Local use)(Running loan)

14 Dividend Warrant

15 Travellers Cheques

16 Demand Draft

18 Gift Cheques

29 At Par Current Account Cheques

30 At Par Cash Credit Account Cheques (Running loan)

31 At Par Saving Bank Cheques

c. Cheque Truncation System (CTS)

Cheque Truncation System (CTS) is a process of presentation of an electronic image of the cheque instead of physical cheque to the Drawee bank through the clearing house. The Reserve Bank of India has implemented CTS in National Capital Region (NCR), New Delhi, Chennai and Mumbai with effect from February 1, 2008, September 24, 2011 and April 27, 2013 respectively. After migration of the entire cheque volume from MICR system for CTS, the traditional MICR-based cheque processing has been discontinued across the country.

Now with the introduction of imaging and truncation, the physical movement of instruments has been stopped. The working of the clearing house has been completely changed with the implementation of CTS. Bank customer stand benefited to a great extent. The following are some of the benefit from the CTS:

    a. Shorter Clearing Cycle

    b. Superior verification and reconciliation process.

    c. No geographical restrictions as to jurisdiction.

    d. Operational efficiency for banks and its customers.

    e. No collection charges for collection of cheque drawn on a bank located within the grid.

d. Indian Financial Code System (IFSC)

IFSC code appearing on the cheque leaves is an eleven digit code with the first 4 alpha characters representing the bank and the last 6 characters representing the branch.

The fifth character is 0 (zero). IFSC code is required when we need to get or transfer funds using NEFT or RTGS system.

12. Other Payment Systems

It is also important to know about the following other type of payment systems/services which are available for making/receiving payment to/from third parties:

a. Electronic Clearing Service (ECS)

ECS is an electronic mode of funds transfer from one bank account to another. It can be used by the institution for making payments such as distribution of dividend interest, salary and pension. It can also be used to pay telephone, electricity and water bill. It is widely used for making payment of Equal Monthly Instalments of loans. It can be used for both credit and debit transactions.

b. National Electronic Fund Transfer (NEFT)

NEFT is a nationwide payment system facilitating the one-to-one transfer. Under this scheme, individual, firms and corporate can electronically transfer funds from any bank branch to any individual, firm and corporate account with any other bank branch in the country participating in this scheme. Under this scheme there is no limit on the amount that could be transferred except maximum of ₹50000/- per transaction for cash based remittances within India. NEFT transactions can be carried not only by visiting the bank branch but also through internet banking. Even one can use ATM to carry out NEFT transactions.

c. Real Time Gross Settlement (RTGS)

It can be defined as the continuous (real time) settlement of funds transfers individually on an order by order (without netting). Presently Rupees Two lakh and above can be remitted under this scheme.

d. Immediate Payment Service (IMPS)

Immediate Payment Service is 24 × 7 **interbank** electronic fund transfer service through mobile phones, internet and ATM. This service was initiated by National Payments Corporation of India in the year 2010.

e. Mobile Wallet

Mobile now can be used as Wallet to make payments of one's purchases. Banks and companies offer digital wallet services in which the user preload money. The preload money can be used to buy goods and services, withdraw cash at ATMs and bank and transfer money to third parties.

13. Cheque Frauds

The use of Cheques in most of the developed/developing countries has declined rapidly over the last few years with the growing popularity of other type of payment instruments such as cards and internet banking. India has also made remarkable progress in the field of electronic banking, however, we still having maximum uses of cheque and it is very important to learn all about cheque fraud.

Fraud or Cheque fraud has not been defined directly in the Indian Penal Code. However, a section dealing with cheating, concealment, forgery, counterfeiting, misappropriation and breach of trust is relevant to book a fraudster.

'Fraud' word has been defined under section 17 of Indian Contract Act. In brief the definition provided therein, mainly includes some acts of dishonesty committed by a party to a contract.

In layman language Bank Fraud is mainly an act of criminals to steal the money from a bank account using different tricks.

Reserve Bank of India in its guidelines on information security, electronic banking, technology management and Cyber frauds has suggested the following about 'Fraud' in the context of electronic banking:

'A deliberate act of omission or commission by any person, carried out in the course of a banking transaction or in the books of accounts maintained manually or under computer system in banks, resulting in a wrongful gain to any person for a temporary period or otherwise, with or without any monetary loss to the bank'

Cheque fraud can also be described as an act of a criminal or a gang of criminals to acquire cheques, provided by the bank to its account holders, and use the same illegally/fraudulently to withdraw money from the account of the account holder of the bank without his knowledge.

The usages of cheques in any form (fake/ clone cheques/cheques of a closed account/using cheques as banker cheque) to cheat individuals can also be described as cheque fraud.

14. Type of Cheque Frauds

The following types of cheque frauds are very common:

   a. Counterfeit Cheques
   b. Stolen Cheques
   c. Altered Cheques
   d. Forged Cheques (signature)
   e. Forged Cheques (endorsement)
   f. Cheques drawn on a closed account
   g. Cheques Drawn as to look like Demand Draft or Banker Cheque

The detail description of the above types of frauds is given hereunder:

a. Counterfeit Cheques

Nowadays it is very easy and possible with the help of sophisticated technology to create a counterfeit cheque. Fraudsters are using sophisticated technology available to make counterfeit cheques. They first collect the relevant information required to create counterfeit cheque and subsequently encash it by transferring the money to their account open with a fake identity.

Counterfeit cheque frauds are most successful as the fraudsters use the best technology to make counterfeit cheques and documents. They also obtain all the information about the victims from one or the other source. These cheques basically have scanned signatures of the victims and the cheque numbers mainly used on the cheques which the culprits ensure that the same have not so far been presented to the bank for payment.

b. Stolen Cheques

The number of stolen cheque cases is growing. Cheques are stolen from the banks drop box or while in transit when the same are sent by courier or by post to the payee. The fraudster opens account in the name of the payee of these stolen cheques by submitting fake identity documents and transfer the proceeds of the cheques into these accounts and subsequently withdraws the same. In case of stolen blank cheques the same are encashed by forging the signature of the drawer. In some of the cases it is also found out that the signature appearing on these stolen cheques does not match with the signature available with the banks and the cheques were paid by the banks due to the negligence of the bank staff handling payment of cheques.

c. Altered Cheques

Cheques are required to have the Date, name of the payee, amount in figure and words filled up by the drawer. The cheques having alteration in any of these columns make the cheque an altered cheque. The fraudster mostly makes alterations in a payee name so that the amount can be collected in the new payee's account. The alteration in the amount is also very common. In these cases the culprit adds appropriate figure to alter the amount of the cheque.

d. Forged Cheques (signature)

Cheques are accepted and paid by the bankers only if the same are signed by the drawer. Cheques signed by other than the drawer are forged cheques.

e. Forged Cheques (endorsement)

Cheques are also accepted and paid by the bankers if the same are endorsed in favour of third parties. Cheques endorsed fraudulently and collected in the account other than the rightful beneficiary fall under this category of fraud.

f. Cheques drawn on a closed account

Culprit cheat the victims by giving them cheques issued from closed accounts.

g. Cheques drawn as to look like Demand Draft or Banker Cheque

This is another way of cheating the victims by issuing them Cheques look like demand draft or banker cheque in consideration of buying goods etc.

15. CASE EVENTS OF CHEQUE FRAUDS

One thing common across all Bank frauds is that the fraudster wants to steal money using different methods. These fraudsters keep changing their place and ways of business. It is important to know about the actions and methods as it will educate us to fight against them and safeguard our hard earned money. Incidents of cheque fraud as given below are based on actual cases handled/ investigated by the author during his time as banker and narrated in a simple way for the understanding of the readers.

Case Event 1: Security cheques misused by employee of Direct Selling Agent (DSA):

Three customers holding current accounts in different branches of the bank complained around the same time, of debit of cheques to their accounts, which had not been issued by them.

On verification it was found that in all three cases, the cheques were fabricated and paid, by transfer, to a woman's newly opened bank account in one of the branches of the same bank. The documents provided by her to the bank, for the opening of the account were also found to be forged and fabricated. She deposited these cheques in two of the bank branches, in a different city, for the transfer of the amount to her account. Once the amount was transferred by the bank to her account, she approached the different branches of the bank, and withdrew the maximum cash from her account and remaining amount through ATM.

Now in this case the following questions come to mind about these cheques:

1. How did this fraudster get information about the cheques?
2. How did the bank clear the fabricated cheques?

On probing further, it was found that the original cheques, in all three cases, were given to a Direct Selling Agent (DSA) dealing in car loans for the bank toward security cheques pertaining to the car loan availed by the three customers. The banks in practice take signed blank cheques. The woman who withdrew the money was reported to be the wife of one of the employees of the DSA who photocopied the cheques and got the counterfeits using readily available technology.

The bank passed the cheques, as they resembled the original. However, the staff in this case should have been careful and avoided the fraud.

Customers should keep the following points in mind to safeguard against such frauds:

- ◄ One should never hand over their financial documents to any DSA of a bank.
- ◄ Always hand over any security cheques to bank staff only against proper acknowledgement.

As far as Banks are concerned, the following precautions can make the system fool proof and prevent such frauds:

- ◄ Bank should have some system to identify cheque numbers of cheques taken by them towards security of loan account. This should be similar to any other type of cheque recording in the customer's account, such as paid or stop payment cheques. This way the system will not be allowed to debit the amount of such fabricated cheques. In the present case, the fraudsters used this shortcoming of the banking system to their advantage.
- ◄ Bank staff should be more careful and alert while processing and passing cheques for newly opened account and while handling "at par" cheques of other cities presented to them for transfer/payment.

Case Event 2: Case of Cheque cloning:

A company operating a Call Center reported to the bank that the cheque issued to one of their ex-staff has been wrongly debited to their account for a higher amount.

On checking the records it was found that the cheque was presented in clearing (CTS) by a bank where the beneficiary maintained his account and the amount so collected/credited had already been withdrawn by its client.

As already mentioned that under CTS clearing the image of the cheque is presented to the drawee bank. The onus of the authenticity of the cheques/instruments lies on the collecting bank as the original instrument is deposited with them for presentation to the drawee bank.

On investigation of this case, the payee informed that he provided the photocopy of the cheque and also his ATM card and PIN to one of his friend who resorted to this mischief. He also disclosed that the original cheque is still in his possession and showed the same to the investigators.

The modus operandi of this gang was that on receipt of the photocopy of the cheque they used the information to fabricate/counterfeit/clone a new cheque for a higher amount and deposited in the account maintained by the ex-staff and withdrew the amount immediately through ATM once the cheque was paid.

It was also observed that the gang used this trick with many other ex-staff of the company. This incident created problems for the ex-employee as he was used by the gang as a front man for this fraud.

Key learning from this:

- ◀ Bank customers should never disclose or share their financial and personal information and any documents with anybody.
- ◀ Companies on their part should pay the dues of their staff or ex-staff by transferring online to their bank accounts or pay the money by means of Banker Cheque/Demand Draft.
- ◀ The banks on their part should strengthen their clearing department and put trained staff to examine any fake and cloned instruments.

Case Event 3: Cheque stolen from Drop Box and misused:

A customer filed a complaint with the bank that although his account had been debited towards one cheque issued by him to one of his suppliers, the supplier did not receive money. On investigation of this case it was observed that on receipt of the cheque the supplier deposited it with his bank by dropping the same into a cheque drop box which was placed in the ATM room of the bank. The cheque was stolen and the culprit opened an account with a bank in the same name (payee) as appearing on the cheque by submitting fake and forged documents. He deposited the cheque in this fake account and withdrew all the money thereafter.

Number of fraud cases of cheques stolen from drop box have been reported. Criminals have used different ways to encash these cheques. In some cases it was observed that cheques were stolen from drop boxes and colour scanned.

Then with the help of sophisticated computer software, all details were erased except the signature and the cheque was fraudulently encashed by adding new information such as payee and amount.

We need to be careful while depositing cheques in the bank branch for the credit of our account and ensure the following:

- ◀ That as far as possible cheques should be deposited at the counter of the bank branch against proper acknowledgement. Banks have been directed by Reserve Bank of India to accept the cheques on their counter from their customers.
- ◀ In case a cheque is to be deposited in a drop box, it must be checked whether the drop box location is safe.
- ◀ As far as banks are concerned they should ensure the safety of their drop boxes and provide this facility in 100% secure locations.

Case Event 4: Cheque leaves removed from cheque book by office staff and misused:

A company, on receipt of cheque books by courier kept them in the office without verifying the contents, such as cheque leaves and requisition slip, etc. After a few days they observed that few cheques which were not issued by them have been debited to their account. The cheques were from one of the cheque books received by them through courier few days ago.

The company reported the matter to the bank and claimed that the cheque leaves must have been removed in transit from the bank to the company's office and asked the bank to investigate and make good the money.

On investigation by the bank it was found that the cheque leaves were removed by one of the office staff of the company and misused.

These type of frauds can be avoided, provided the customers ensure that:

- On receipt of the cheque book, verify that all cheque leaves are available in the cheque book.
- The cheque books should always be kept in a safe place and in dual control.

Case Event 5: Extra cheque obtained by the Staff of DSA and misused:

When we avail loans for Vehicle, Housing or any other use we need to provide cheques toward Equal Monthly Instalments (EMI). Canvassing of these types of loans is mainly done by staff of Direct Selling Agents (DSA) appointed by banks. In most cases they assist banks in completing all formalities including collection of advance cheques toward EMIs.

In some cases it was observed that staff of DSAs collect one extra cheque from the borrower and encash the same fraudulently. As per process banks require Cheques to be written in their favour e.g. ABCD Bank Loan A/C NO.1234 toward EMI. However in most of the cases DSA staff take cheques written in the name of the bank only.

Cheques equal to the number of EMIs are to be collected from customers. For loan cases where the first instalment is to be paid along with the margin money or down payment, one less cheque is to be collected i.e. against a loan of 36 months tenure; one is required to give 35 cheques. So in this case these culprits collected 36 cheques and misused the extra cheque by adding the name of one of their staff to make the cheque payable to him i.e. ABCD Bank a/c XYZ. Subsequently they encashed the same as mentioned above.

In number of cases dishonest DSA staff succeeds in cheating bank customers as the latter are unaware of the possibility of being cheated in such a manner. Customers also do not object to a debit of the cheque thinking that the cheque is towards first EMI of their loan account as it is encashed immediately after disbursement of the loan. The bank also honours and pays the cheque as it is presented to them in order.

To avoid such type of frauds we need to keep the following points in mind:

- We must be alert in dealing with DSAs of banks and must clarify each and every aspect and terms of the sanction of loan.
- Hand over the cheques to bank staff only.
- Never issue cheques favouring bank's name only. Add your name or a/c number of loan a/c after the name of the bank.
- It is always advisable to pay EMI using Electronic Clearing Service (ECS) facility instead of issuing cheques. ECS facility is an electronic mode of funds transferred from one bank account to

another bank. We need to provide our mandate and authorization to the bank for this service.

◀ Bank staff should take extra precaution to pass cheques which are issued in their name. In fact, banks should have a policy to refer the cheques to senior level officers where the cheques are issued favouring Bank a/c XYZ.

◀ The reader of this book who might have availed loans in a similar way through DSAs must check this aspect. One can verify from their statement of account by counting total number of EMIs debited to their account.

Case Event 6: Allowing others to use your account can be risky:

Three high value cheques, issued by a corporate were deposited in the bank for transfer of the amount to the credit of saving account of three different individuals maintaining account in three different outstation branches. The cheques were identified as forged cheques by the bank staff and dishonoured.

Although there was no financial loss still it was decided to investigate this case. On investigation of one of the account holder it was observed that four individuals were involved. The involvement and role played by each of the individuals is narrated hereunder which will make one understand the modus operandi of such culprits:

Individual No.1. (The account holder in whose account the cheque was deposited) On investigation the account holder disclosed that he was asked by his friend to receive a payment in his account. The friend in this case mentioned that he does not have an account and requested if individual no. 1 will accept a cheque in his name and deposit in his account. The account holder agreed and subsequently allowed his friend to deposit the cheques in his account.

Individual No. 2. (Friend of individual No.1) On investigation he disclosed that he was asked by one of his friend to identify someone who had a savings account in a particular bank in whose name the cheque can be received and deposited. The objective then was to withdraw the money on realisation of the cheques.

Individual No. 3. (Friend of individual No. 2) On investigation he informed that he was also helping one of his friend who offered him commission for his help to get some of the cheques encashed by depositing the same in an account maintained with one particular bank and he asked his other friend to help him in this matter.

Individual No. 4. (Friend of Individual No.3) Master mind behind the attempted fraud was a Franchise of a leading company. He was the proprietor of the franchise and disclosed having altered cheque, originally issued in favour of other individual, received by him for delivering to the original beneficiaries from his parent company. He asked his friend to identify someone in whose account the cheque could be collected. On identification of the account the cheque was altered and the name of the payee changed. The altered cheque was subsequently deposited in the account of the individual No. 1 for payment. He also disclosed having adopted the similar modus operandi for other two cheques.

It was also observed that the individual mentioned at Sl. No. 1 and 2 were not having any knowledge of the fraud and were simply helping without any financial consideration in good faith. In view of the above one should learn the following tips to avoid falling prey to such frauds:

- Should never allow anybody to use one's bank account as one is running a risk of becoming a party to such frauds. In case of any financial loss the account holder whose account has been used for deposit of fraudulent instruments will be held responsible to make good the money and may face legal action.
- Corporates should always have a system of timely follow up for all cheques issued by them. It is always better to switch over to online banking for all business payments to avoid such threats.

Case Event 7: Do not leave unnecessary space/gaps while writing cheque:

A Corporate account holder used to withdraw ₹7000/- cash from their current account every week for their day to day requirements. The cashier of the company used to write the cheques and also visit the bank to withdraw money. After some time he thought of making quick money by fraudulent means by duping the employer. He learned the trick of writing the cheque by giving sufficient space after the first word of "seven "as well as before the figure 7. The cheque issued originally for ₹7000/- fraudulently was altered to ₹17000/- by adding the word "teen" after seven (seventeen) and 1 before the figure 7000

(17000). So he fraudulently withdrew ₹10000/-more on each transaction. In this way he withdrew a total sum of ₹40000/- in a month. This fraud came to the notice of the company only after a period of more than one year. More than 50 transactions of this type were carried out in the said account during this period.

In view of the above it is very important to take the following precautions to avoid such incidents:

- The role of all the individuals, handling financial transactions should be properly defined.
- Job rotation of the staff should be carried out frequently.
- The person who signs the cheques should always be alert and vigilant while doing so. He must be able to detect any irregularity.
- Bank officials should also be more careful and must always apply an analytical approach while passing the cheques.

Case Event 8: Avoid attractive loan offers:

A number of customers reported to their respective banks that they have been cheated by a gang of criminals whom they approached in response to an advertisement in a Newspaper.

The modus operandi adopted by this gang was to first advertise in newspapers as a finance company providing education and personal loan to individuals. Thereafter when prospect customers approached them, they sanctioned the loan on very easy terms after getting all the personal documents as well as financial information.

They also collected cheques towards EMIs along with a separate cheque towards processing charges and margin money. They assured all that the cheque towards loan amount will be sent to them by courier only after the clearance of cheques taken toward processing charges and margin money.

They collected the money towards processing charges and margin money in cash or by cheque from people who approached them for loans. The cheques given to these people for the loan amount were subsequently dishonoured.

The victims could not contact the culprits as the culprits became unreachable. The victims visited the fake financial company office only to find it closed. On verification from their bankers it was found that all the money received in these accounts had been withdrawn. On further verification it was also found that the culprits opened their account with fake documents.

In view of the above one must follow the tips mentioned below:

- One should always be careful while approaching people in response to such advertisements. Many such advertisements are reported to be placed by criminal gangs.
- If the offer of loan is very attractive than the possibility of being cheated is higher. One must discuss with their bankers or some other established financial institution about such offers.

◀ Banker in this case opened the account of the gang without verifying the genuineness of the documents submitted by them and needed to be alert to the possibility of fraud.

Case Event 9: Using other's pen for writing cheques is very risky:

A company having its showroom in the outskirts of one of the main cities reported to their bank that they had issued a Cheque for ₹100/- in favour of a mobile company, however the same has been debited to their account for Rupees 353000/- (amount changed).

On investigation, it was found that a person visited the showroom of the victim and introduced himself as an employee of a telephone company. He discussed the possibility of installing a mobile tower on the rooftop of the show room at a lucrative monthly rental with the owner of the showroom. The owner agreed and handed over copies of the ownership documents to the fraudster. The fraudster also obtained a cheque of Rupees 100/- in the name of his mobile company on the pretext of verification of signature. The fraudster left the showroom after collecting all the above documents.

The modus operandi adopted by the fraudster in this case was that he asked the victims to sign the cheque while he would fill the remaining details in the presence of the victim. However, the fraudster used a magic pen i.e. a pen with ink that can be erased subsequently.

The fraudster subsequently erased the name of the payee and the amount, refilled the cheque amount and his name as payee, and collected the amount by presenting the same to a branch of the same bank in the main city. He withdrew the maximum amount by cash from the bank and balance through ATM.

A good number of people in small cities become victim of such frauds. In some cases fraudsters first advertised in newspapers to target victims.

One should keep the following in mind to avoid such frauds:

- Never use someone else's pen to write a cheque or allow others to write your cheques.
- One must learn the art of postponing immediate decisions where some unknown persons offer some immediate financial gain.
- Never issue or hand over a cheque to any unknown person.
- Banks must have the expertise to identify the cheques written with Magic Pen.

Case Event 10: Check with banks for non-receipt of your interest payments:

A senior citizen reported that he was getting quarterly payment of interest on his fixed deposit from a bank by means of their banker cheque. When in one quarter the same was not received he went to the bank to inquire for the same. The bank officials after checking their records informed him that the banker cheque has already been sent to him in time and they have already paid the same. On verification it was found that this time the banker cheque was presented and paid to some other bank.

On investigating this case it was found that the Banker cheque in question was received by the son of the senior citizen and deposited to an account opened by the son in the name of the father by using forged documents.

In view of the above one needs to:

- ◄ Be alert and track all payments due to them.
- ◄ Banks, also must advise their customers to opt for ECS option to get such payments.

16. How to avoid Cheque Frauds

The best way to avoid any fraud is to be alert and careful while handling any financial transaction. We must also ensure all our financial documents are kept or stored safely and never share our financial information with any unknown person.

The possibility of cheque fraud starts with the issuance of cheque book to account holders by the bank. Safekeeping of cheque book as well as learning the safe way to write cheques is very important. All these and other safety measures are discussed subsequently in detail.

17. Safety of Cheque Book

Cheque Book as mentioned earlier is provided by banks to its customers when they open their account or when they place a request for a new cheque book. Cheque books contain 10/25/100 Cheque leaves and are delivered to the account holder either in person or by post. Banks can also hand over the cheque book to the authorized person of the account holder. A cheque book also contains a Requisition

Slip that is required to be sent to the bank to get a new cheque book. Safety of cheque book is very important and customers should take the following steps to avoid cheque frauds:

a. Verify and count all the cheque leaves

In a number of instances of Cheque frauds it is observed that the cheque leaves are removed from the cheque books when the same are in transit from the bank to the place of the account holder. It is therefore necessary to ensure that all the cheque leaves are intact as soon as one receives the cheque book. In case a cheque leave is missing, immediately inform the bank and ask them to take a stop payment request of the missing cheque leaves. The same can also be done using internet banking. This will ensure 100% safety as the customer would be able to know the status of the cheque and be able to mark the stop payment sitting at any place and that too round the clock.

b. Keep the cheque book in a safe place

Never leave your cheque book in your vehicle or any other place that can be accessed by unknown people. Keep the same in a safe place.

c. Follow your cheque book when in transit

In a number of cases it is observed that the cheque books are stolen in transit from the bank to the customers place and misused. One must check with the Bank if the Cheque Book has not been received within a reasonable time from submitting the requisition slip for a new cheque book. In case the cheque book is not received take up the matter with your bank to know the status.

d. Record of cheques issued

Account holders must always keep a full record of the cheques issued either on the record slip available in the cheque book or on a separate file. In case any of the unused cheque leaf is missing the bank must be immediately informed to stop payment against the missing cheque.

e. Stop Payment of unused Cheques

Write to your Banker to mark stop payment on all the unused Cheques in case the Cheque Book is misplaced.

f. Safe Custody of Cheque Book

In number of fraud cases it is observed that known person to the victim, either some relative at home or some office staff at office, steals/remove few cheque leaves of the cheque book and withdraw fraudulently the money from the account. The cheque book must be kept in the safe custody all the time.

18. Cheque Requisition Slip

Cheque Requisition Slip is a very important document as banks are issuing cheque book on receiving the same from their customers. In a number of frauds it was observed that the fraudsters got the cheque books issued from the banks after acquiring the cheque requisition slips of their customers and then fraudulently withdrew money. It is therefore necessary to protect and ensure the safekeeping of the Cheque Requisition Slip. So whenever one gets a new cheque book it is very important to check that the cheque requisition slip is available in the Cheque Book. In case the cheque requisition slip is not available one must inform the bank immediately by email and also in writing.

19. Writing the Cheque

One should be careful while writing cheques. Cheques written perfectly minimize the risk of cheque fraud.

Users must take the following precautions while writing a cheque:

1. Fill all the contents, such as date, name of the payee, amount in words and figures, in the cheque properly and carefully.
2. Always use black or blue ball pen or a pen with indelible ink.
3. Ensure that no large blank space is left before the start of the amount in words and figure lines to avoid a fraudster from adding any figure or word to alter the amount of the cheque.
4. Suffix "/-"after the amount written in figures. I. e. ₹10000 as ₹10000/-.
5. Always use your own pen to write cheques. Writing cheques using a pen given by another person is very risky as it may be a magic pen the ink of which can be erased to alter the contents of the cheque.
6. Never give a signed blank cheque to anybody.

7. Never keep a signed blank cheque. First fill the cheque and sign the cheque only after verifying that all the details filled in the cheque are in order.
8. Must cross your cheque properly whenever required. If the cheque is to be sent by post must ensure to cross the same putting two parallel lines on the left side upper corner of the cheque or write "Account Payee Only" written in between the parallel lines to make it more secure.
9. Must draw lines on the unused space after the payee name and amount in figures.
10. The word "or bearer" printed on the cheque leaves at the end of the line start with "Pay to" allow the person who carries the cheque for receiving payment.
11. Never erase any mistake on a cheque and issue fresh cheque in case of any mistake.
12. Ensure not to alter or overwrite while writing a cheque. Always issue a fresh cheque in such cases.
13. Never write or sign on the MIRC band (bottom of the cheque)
14. Destroy all cancelled cheques. While closing an account any unused cheques linked to that account should also be destroyed.
15. Ensure to write CANCEL across the face of the cheque if you are required to give a blank cheque to any agency for ECS purpose. Must write the name of the agency on the back of the cheque and also write the purpose. Score out the cheque number before handing over the cheque.

20. Other Precautions

Apart from handling, safe keeping of cheque book and the writing of cheques, bank customers must learn the art of safe banking. Banks at their end issue alerts, tips and guidelines, from time to time, to their customers so that they do not become victims of bank frauds.

The following tips will help you practice safe baking:

1. Never issue cheques in favour of an unknown person. The person may be a fraudster and may misuse the cheque.

2. One must register their mobile number with the banker and avail all facilities of SMS alerts provided by banks. In case of cheques the Reserve Bank of India has already issued preventive measures guidelines to all banks and specifically asked them to send SMS alert to its customers on their mobile whenever cheques are received in clearing. All such alerts from banks must be given due priority and read immediately. If one observes debit of any unauthorized cheque, immediately inform the bank. Timely action from the customer, in case of presentation of any fraudulent cheque, can avoid the fraud and loss of money.

3. One must review his bank account statement regularly or check all the transactions through online or telephone banking. In case of any doubtful transaction, notify the bank immediately.

4. One must keep track of all cheques issued by him or sent to others to ensure that the same have been received by them. Immediately take up cases with

your banker where the cheques have not been received by the recipient and find out the status. Issue another cheque only after stopping payment of the earlier cheque.

5. Learn and consider other electronic payment methods such as NEFT/RTGS etc. as they are more secure than cheques.

6. One should never disclose their personal and financial information such as date of birth, address, bank account number, ATM/Credit card number and PIN over the phone to anybody known or unknown person or in response to any email received.

21. Precautionary Tips on Receiving and Accepting Cheques/Bankers Cheques/ Drafts from others

So far we have covered safe keeping of cheque books and writing of cheques whereas one also receives cheques from other issued in their favour. So one is not only issuing/writing cheques, but also receives cheques.

Remember that one is responsible for all the cheques deposited in their account. The banks are providing uncleared balance against these cheques till the same are paid and you may be provided access to the funds against the uncleared balance. The amount credited in the account against the clearing cheques with value date can be removed from the account if the cheque is found to be fraudulent. It is therefore very important to be equally careful while accepting cheques, banker cheques and drafts from others.

The following precautionary tips should be followed when receiving/accepting cheques, demand drafts or other cheques from others:

1. Cheques and bankers' cheques/demand drafts can be altered or forged, so never accept the same from **unknown persons**. If received otherwise one must check with their banker about the genuineness of the instrument before parting with any kind of material or items for which the instrument is issued to you. In number of fraud cases it is observed that fraudsters first win the confidence of the shopkeeper or supplier by purchasing small valuable items on cash basis and thereafter try to take high value items against the forged cheques or drafts, so never supply any item without confirming the genuineness of the instrument. It will be more appropriate to hand over the material only once the proceeds of the cheque or draft has been credited to your account. It is always safer to ask for online payment.
2. One should never allow anybody to use their account or accept payment via cheque or other instrument on someone else's behalf. In most of such cases the fraudster encash forged cheques through third party.
3. As far as possible Accept only CTS-2010 compliant cheques.
4. One must try to refuse post-dated cheques.
5. One should not accept cheques issued originally in favour of another individual and then endorsed

in your favour. As per practice, banks accept such type of cheques only when the endorsement on the cheque is confirmed by you. Confirming any endorsement makes you liable for any defect in the cheque. One can get in trouble in case the cheque is subsequently found to be forged.

6. One should track all cheques which are sent to you and are in transit. Non receipt or delay in receipt of any such cheque should be taken up immediately with the person/organization that sent you the cheque.

7. Never accept cheques that have been altered. Reserve Bank of India has issued strict instructions prohibiting alterations or corrections on cheques to be cleared through Cheque Truncation System. This has been done only to curtail cheque related frauds. No changes or corrections can be carried out on cheques other than for date validation purposes.

8. Cheques/Banker Cheques/Demand Drafts have security features. It is mandatory for banks to print cheques that carry a standardized Watermark called "CTS-INDIA" which can only be seen when you hold the cheque against light. This feature will make it difficult for fraudsters to use photocopies of the cheques. It is important to check this when one receives a cheque.

22. Precautionary Tips for Bank Staff handling Cheque Transactions

Bank staff plays a vital role in protecting our money and it is true to say that an alert and careful bank staff can challenge fraudsters and defeat them in their efforts to steal our money. Therefore, the main objective of bank staff should not be only to solve fraud cases or recover money, but also to instill fear among those doing fraudulent activities. Fraudsters should be made to realize that there is strict and systematic arrangement within banks to fence the fraud.

In the previous chapters most aspects of a cheque have been covered. The aspect of Categorizations of cheques received for payment by banks based on their functionality like Cash Cheques, Transfer Cheques, Clearing Cheques and Local/Outstation cheques has also been covered.

Banks get a number of fraudulent instruments for payment every day. While majority of such cases are identified and fraud prevented some still go unspotted. On looking at most of the cases of cheque frauds the author is of the opinion that the same could have been avoided with little more alertness of bank staff. It is very important that in case of any apprehension or uncertainty about any aspect, the cheque should not be passed for lack of time or for any other compelling reasons. Bank staff must be completely satisfied about the genuineness and validity of the cheque. Banks should have a team of experts who should be given the responsibility of analyzing and reviewing any doubtful instruments.

It is also very important that banks should also have multiple level checks, above a threshold limit depending upon the volume of cheque business.

The following are some of the precautionary tips for Bank staff for handling payment and collection of cheques.

These precautions relate to inward and outward clearing transactions and may be applied to all types of cheque payments and handling of cheques drawn on other banks:

a. Inward Clearing Cheques (Paying Bank)

1. With the introduction of the Cheque Truncation System banks receive the electronic image of a truncated cheque. The bank staff handling these images are required to be well trained and must know all processes related to handling inward clearing as given in the Cheque Truncation System. The bank staff must also know the relevant clauses of the amended Negotiable Instruments Act, 1881.

2. Bank staff should be alert while handling Inward Clearing cheques transactions. Spending a little extra time to examine any cheque can be of great value.

3. Examine the instruments carefully **for**:

    a. **Signatures.** Verify the signatures with the specimen signature available in the bank records In case of any doubt; it is always better to contact the customer to check in case of any doubt. In case the customer confirms the signatures, then ask him to provide new set of specimen signatures.

    b. **Date of issue** to verify the validity of the instruments.

    c. The **amount written in words and figures** to verify whether the same is matched with each other.

    d. **Correction/alteration/addition** (on the face as well as on the back side of the cheque).

e. **Cheques issued as DD/PO style.** To verify their transaction code numbers.

f. Examine **the gaps** in writing. Irregular gaps must be examined with more care.

g. Examine **the endorsement** of the presenting bank and ensure that the same is in order.

h. Ensure that the cheque is **not endorsed to two banks.**

4. Check with the customer, over **registered mobile phone** and not the one mentioned on the back side of the cheque, before passing the cheques in the below mentioned scenarios:

    a. **Different ink** is used in multiple places writing the cheque.

    b. If issued in the **name of presenting bank A/c xyz**.

    c. **High value cheques** issued in the name of any individual.

    d. In cases of **cheques drawn from newly opened Accounts**.

5. Return the instruments bearing **alterations** with the reason "Alteration not allowed". However, please note that Alteration on date is allowed provided the same is authenticated with full signatures of the drawer.

6. Never pay **doubtful instruments**. In case of any doubt the cheque should be referred to the senior officer.

7. While returning the cheques to the presenting bank ensure that the **reason of return** should be as per the list of return reasons prescribed by Reserve Bank of India.

b. Outward Clearing Cheques (Presenting Bank)

Presently, since the payment processing is done on the basis of cheques images and in view of the amendment of section 131 of the negotiable instrument act, the onus of due diligence has been shifted to the presenting bank. It is therefore very important to verify the prima facie genuineness of the cheque to be truncated and any fraud, forgery or tampering apparent on the face of the instrument that can be verified with due diligence and ordinary care.

The following few tips must be followed while handling outward clearing cheques:

1. Must know about the **security features**, such as watermark etc. on the cheques. Must verify the same while processing the cheques.
2. Examine the instruments carefully for:
   a. Style of Signatures.
   b. Date of issue.
   c. The amount written in words and figures.
   d. Cheques issued as DD/PO.
   e. Stationary.
   f. Security features.
   g. Gaps in writing.
   h. Different ink is used in writing the cheque.
   i. High value cheque issued in the name of any individual.
3. Do not present for payment any instruments bearing alterations or corrections. However,

Instruments having alteration of its date is allowed provided the drawer authenticates the same with full signatures.

4. In case of any doubt of any nature while handling any type of instrument must discuss with the senior officer. In case it is required must talk to the customer as he is the best person to clear the doubts.

5. Must Use ultra violet lamp to verify cheques. In most cases, the fraud is perpetrated by altering the cheques in one or the other way. Ultra-violet lamp helps to identify tampering in a cheque, making fraud detection very easy.

SECTION 2

ATM/DEBIT/CREDIT CARD FRAUDS

1. The Need and importance of Cards (ATM/Debit/Credit Cards)

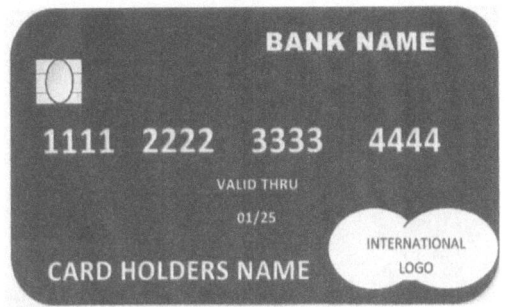

Cards play a very important role in our financial transactions. Most people use cards almost every day. Banks also encourage use of cards as the customer is able to carry out financial transactions without visiting a branch which means lower costs for both the bank and its customers. Card users also have great advantages as they can access banking services 24/7. It is necessary to know about the various types of cards available for our use and other important information relating to them.

2. Classification of Cards

Cards can be classified into three types according to their usages:

a. ATM/Debit Cards

ATM/Debit cards are linked to the bank account of the client, mostly used up to the balance available in the customer's account. ATM card is mostly used for cash withdrawals at ATMs whereas a debit card can be used for cash withdrawals at ATMs as well as for purchases online and on retail outlets for the purchase of goods and services. The customer's account is debited on usage of the ATM/Debit Card for such transactions.

b. Credit Cards

Credit Cards are mostly not linked to the bank account of the customer. These cards are issued by banks and other financial agencies to its customers to enable them to shop on credit basis for a short period at various channels specifically at Point of sale. The holder of a credit card can also withdraw cash from any ATM as per the arrangement and cash limit fixed by the card issuing bank/agency.

c. Prepaid Cards

Prepaid Cards are issued by the banks and other financial agencies for a fixed sum of money against the value paid in advance by the card holder. These cards can be used not only for cash withdrawal but also for other purposes such as purchase of goods and services. Travel and Gift cards fall under this category.

3. Other Important Information about Cards

a. Visa/Master Card/Maestro

All types of cards carry the logos of the international payment systems i.e. Visa, Master Card or Maestro, who license their brands to member financial institutions that in turn provide services to the consumers and merchants. Cards carrying these logos can mostly be used worldwide.

b. RuPay Cards

Similar to Visa, Master Card/Maestro, international payment systems, RuPay is an Indian domestic card payment scheme launched by National Payments Corporation of India (NPCI). This is presently used in India only.

c. International usages of Cards

Debit/Credit cards can be used both domestically and internationally. Banks need to enable the cards for international usages. In India the banks are authorised by the Reserve Bank of India to issue debit and credit cards only for domestic usage unless international use is specifically requested by the customer.

d. Personal Identification Number (PIN)

A PIN is a password provided by the banks or other agencies initially by which the card (ATM/Debit/Credit Card) is issued. The PIN is also provided for other online services availed by the individual. The PIN is subsequently required to be changed by the individual to ensure secrecy of the same. The PIN is a proof of the ownership/identification of the card holder for the usage of the card or for any other specific online services for which the same is created. In India, the cardholder is required to enter the PIN to complete the card transactions.

e. One Time Password (OTP)

OTP is an additional fence for protection sent by the service providers on one's registered mobile and email id or one of these as opted for by the customer. The OTP can be used only once and expires within a prescribed time limit if not used. The OTP typically follows the regular PIN or password and serves as the users' second password. OTP is mostly provided in cases of selective online transactions and not necessary for each and every transaction. This is mainly to prevent misuse of your login.

f. Credit Verification Value (CVV)

CVV is a three digit number printed on the back side of Debit/Credit card on the signature strip. This is required to be furnished to the online merchants to complete online financial transactions through debit or credit card. Furnishing CVV number proves that the card owner is in possession of the card. CVV is also known as Card Security Code (CSC).

4. How to use Cards

With the growth in the number of transactions associated with all types of cards frauds are also on the rise. Every day we come across some news of fraud relating to card transactions. Most of these frauds take place when one uses these cards at Automated Teller Machine (ATM) booths for withdrawal of cash and at Point of Sale locations for purchase of goods and services. It is therefore very important to know about Automated Teller Machine (ATM) and Point of Sale (POS) terminals where the cards are used most frequently. The information as provided subsequently will help to understand the functioning of cards and also reduce risk of frauds.

5. Automated Teller Machine (ATM)

Automated Teller Machine is a computerized machine that provides customers of banks the facility of accessing their account by putting their ATM/Debit card in the ATM to undertake the following financial and non-financial transactions, round the clock, without visiting the bank:

- a. Cash Withdrawal
- b. Cash Deposit
- c. Balance Enquiry
- d. Mini Statement of account
- e. Fund Transfer
- f. Cheque Book request
- g. Statement Request
- h. PIN Change
- i. Credit Card Payment
- j. Mobile Recharge
- k. Update personal information

6. White Label ATM (WLA)

The Reserve Bank of India, vide its notification issued in the year 2012 permitted non-bank entities incorporated in India under the Companies Act 1956, to set up, own up, own and operate ATMs in India. These type of ATMs permitted by the Reserve Bank of India are known as White Label ATM. Tata Communication

Payment Solutions Ltd launched the first White Label ATM on 27 June 2013 in Mumbai. The customers of the banks in India can avail specific banking services through their cards (Debit/Credit/Prepaid) issued to them by their banks on these White Label ATMs.

7. Location wise Classification of Automated Teller Machine (ATM)

a. **On-site:** ATM situated within the branch premises or very close to the branch premises.

b. **Off-site/premises:** ATM situated far from the branch of the account holder at various places like shopping centers, petrol pumps, railway stations and airports.

c. **Work-site:** ATM situated within an establishment or organization for the use of their staff.

d. **ATM on wheels:** ATM that moves to different places for the use of the customers of the bank as well as for the cardholders of other banks.

8. Type of Cards used at an ATM

The following cards issued by banks and other authorized agencies can be used at an ATM for various transactions:

1. ATM Cards
2. ATM cum Debit Cards
3. Credit Cards
4. Travel Cards
5. Gift Cards

Credit Cards, Travel Cards and Gift Cards can be used at an ATM only for withdrawal of Cash.

9. Advantage of ATMs

The introduction of ATM in the banking sector has completely changed its working and brought multiple benefits for its customers. The benefits for the banks and its customers are given subsequently in detail in point number 10 and 11.

10. Banks Advantages

a. Reduced workload in the bank branches. The focus changed to other profitable areas.
b. The efficiency of staff in the bank branches increased.
c. Extension of working hours by way of a 24 × 7 access model. ATM machines are available 24 × 7 365 days, enabling banks to provide various services without any break.
d. Operating expenses reduced as opening and managing branches is more expensive than providing ATM services at locations where banks can get business without having full-fledged branches.
e. Enhanced the presence of banks.
f. ATM enabled a "working smart" model hence enhancing the reputation of banks.

11. Customers Advantages

a. 24 × 7 365 days availability of banking services.
b. Customers can also use the ATM of other banks.
c. ATMs are set up in almost all-important residential and commercial areas, making it very easy for the user to access the same as per their convenience.
d. Saves travel time.
e. Less risk of carrying cash from a distance.
f. Avoidance of crowded branches.

g. Getting quick and efficient service.
h. Security and privacy ensured.
i. Getting new or clean currency notes.

12. Comparison of ATM Card with a Debit Card and a Credit Card

Comparison	ATM Card	Debit Card	Credit Card
Payment terms	Withdrawal from ATM leads to a simultaneous debited to the card holders' Bank account linked to the Card.	Purchases of goods and services made over POS terminal, usages for online purchases and withdrawal from an ATM is simultaneously debited to card holder's Bank account linked to the Card.	Purchase of goods and services made over POS terminal, usages for online purchases and withdrawal from the ATM are on short term credit basis and to be paid on due date as per the arrangement.
Bank Account	Need to have account with the card issuing bank.	Need to have account with the card issuing bank.	Not necessary to have an accounts with the card-issuing agency.
Card Limit	Up to the available balance in the linked account.	Up to the available balance in the linked account.	AS per the Limit fixed by the credit card issuing bank/ agency.

13. How to Operate Automated Teller Machine (ATM)?

ATMs are available 24/7 at most locations and used by all the cardholders irrespective of the bank in which they maintain account. It is very easy to operate and convenient for the cardholders to access their bank account from any ATM. More and more people are using ATMs regularly. Therefore, it is very important to know how to use an ATM. We must know about the following components of the ATM machines mostly used by us:

a. Card Slot/Card Reader
b. Display Screen
c. Keypad
d. Screen Buttons
e. Cash Dispenser
f. Receipt Printer
g. Speaker

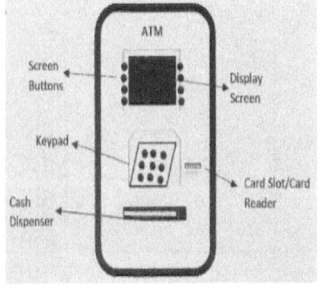

As already mentioned, it is very easy to operate an ATM machine. Immediately after inserting the card into the card slot, the ATM machine starts communicating or displaying further operations/actions required to be undertaken by the cardholder. The communication is not only through the speaker, but also displayed on the ATM screen. The cardholder has to listen or read the directions carefully and follow the same. The cardholder needs to press the button next to the indicated option. In case the

ATM has a touch screen facility the cardholder needs to press the screen based on the various transaction options.

14. Stepwise process of operating the ATM

The following are some of the options, which one needs to perform mostly for the withdrawal of cash. The other options such as change of password, transfer of funds, balance enquiry etc. are also available:

Step	Action	Remarks
Step 1	Insert your Card in the card slot.	Card readers are mostly two types. In some machines, the machine swallows the card and returns it after disbursing cash. In others, the dip- card reader works, where one needs to insert the card, remove the same immediately, and follow the menu options displayed on the ATM screen. Most banks use Dip-card readers.
Step 2	Select Your Language.	This option appears on the ATM screen with options of few languages. The cardholder need to select one of the languages.
Step 3	Enter your PIN and Press proceed button.	This option appears on the ATM screen. The cardholder needs to enter the correct PIN using the keypad and needs to press the indicated button to proceed. If an incorrect PIN is entered the machine will request the card holder to enter the correct PIN.

Step 4	Select your option for the transaction.	The ATM screen shows the options of various transactions such as Withdrawal, Balance Enquiry, Mini statement and PIN change etc. Cardholder needs to select as per his requirement by pressing the button next to the required option. In case you select the withdrawal option, follow step 5 below for next options.
Step 5	Select type of your account option.	Cardholder needs to select the type of account from the options of Saving, Current and Credit Card displayed on the ATM screen by pressing the button next to it.
Step 6	Enter amount.	Cardholder needs to enter or type the amount to be withdrawn using the keypad and then press the button "Correct" if the amount displayed on the screen matches with what has been entered. In some ATMs, other options such as Fast Cash and favoured cash are also displayed.
Step 7	Do you want a receipt for this transaction?	Cardholder needs to select from yes or no option displayed on the screen.
Step 8	Wait while your transaction is being processed.	Cardholder needs to wait and collect the amount immediately when dispensed by an ATM machine. ATM machine will also dispense the Receipt if selected yes for the same by the cardholder.

15. Failed Transactions-Account debited cash not disbursed

It is very important to know that when one uses an ATM, sometime, the account is debited but cash is not disbursed. One must lodge a complaint with the card-issuing bank for the same immediately, but not later than 30 days of the date of transaction. As per the Reserve Bank of India guidelines, the concerned bank must attend such complaints on priority basis and refund the amount within 7 days from the date of receipt of the complaint.

16. What to do in case your card is Stuck in ATM

It is very common and many of us have faced a situation where our card was stuck inside the ATM.

The card can be stuck in the machine mainly due to two reasons, first, delay in entering details and second, due to some technical reasons.

In a situation like this immediately inform your bank giving full details of the ATM location and **block the card so that it is not misused by anybody.**

17. ATM operational Complaints

With a large network of ATMs all over India, the following are some of the common user complaints. These complaints have also been identified and reviewed by the Reserve Bank of India:

    a. Frequently Breakdown of machines

    b. Discrepancies in cash dispensation

c. Machine running out of cash
d. Quality of Notes
e. Grievance Redressal
f. Lack of security arrangement
g. Cash not received, but account debited

18. Card Frauds-ATM Frauds

Card frauds occur when a person other than the card owner uses the card without his permission.

ATM fraud can be defined in different ways but the outcome of such fraud is common i.e. of cheating and stealing money by the perpetrator from the account of the cardholder/victim by using different means.

Since 1967 when the first Automated Teller Machine (ATM) was installed the perpetrators started their efforts not only to steal the cash kept in the ATM machine, but also resorted to other fraudulent ways to withdraw money from the bank accounts of genuine card holders by using the ATM channel.

ATM frauds are possible only when the perpetrator acquires personal information of the card holder, such as Card number and Personal Identification Number (PIN).

Increase in number of ATM frauds is a great concern for all of us. Almost every day we read in the newspapers about one or the other incident of ATM frauds. During the last few years I have been looking closely into most of the news about ATM frauds and have regularly explained preventive measures on social media platforms like

Facebook and LinkedIn for the benefit of my friends. I also personally handled ATM fraud cases referred to me by a number of ATM fraud victims.

In my view, most of the ATM frauds can be avoided with awareness and alertness.

19. Type of ATM frauds

Perpetrator always tries different tricks to acquire financial as well as personal information of the individuals. They use the same to fraudulently withdraw money from our bank account. Withdrawal of money from ATM fraudulently is known as ATM frauds. The following types of ATM frauds are very common:

a. Card Theft

Card theft can be categorised into the following different ways:

1. **Physical Theft**: Where the perpetrator takes the physical possession of the card from the card holder by stealing the same either from his possession or from other locations where the card is kept by the card holder.
2. **Card Trapping**: One of very common method to steal an ATM/Debit card. This method is known as Lebanese loop. In this method the perpetrator fixes a device in the card entry slot in a way that it allows the user to enter the card, but prevents the ATM card reader from ejecting the card. Once the card holder leaves, the fraudster can take out the card and use it.

3. **Card Swapping/Switching:** This is another method of card theft where the card of the user is exchanged with a fake card of a similar appearance. In such cases of card theft, the perpetrator targets a user who is facing some problem in operating the ATM. They offer them help, and once one agrees they divert their attention and exchange their cards.

b. Personal Identification Number (PIN) Stealing

Money from an ATM can only be withdrawn on entering a valid PIN after inserting the ATM card. So to complete any ATM transaction one needs to have a valid PIN. The perpetrators use various methods to steal/acquire ATM PINs. **Shoulder Surfing** is one of the easiest ways to steal the PIN. In this method the perpetrator stands very close to the card holder to watch and copy the numbers pressed by him to enter the PIN on the keypad.

c. Card Skimming

Skimming can be defined as fraudulently stealing card detail, such as PIN and account detail. The perpetrator uses different devises to capture the PIN and card data and subsequently loads it into a fake card to access the card holder's money. Skimming is often done by organized gangs who place a skimming device near the ATM in such a way that the user can't spot about their presence easily. The skimmers sometimes place a secondary keypad on top of the existing keypad. The secondary keypad captures the PIN number when the same is entered by the user.

20. Important Tips to Safeguard from ATM/Debit/Credit Card Frauds

Protection of our personal and financial information as well as the security of our cards/Chequebooks and other financial documents is very important to avoid any type of bank fraud. Culprits acquire this information using different tricks. Most popular tricks is known as **Phishing** which is a type of fraud in which the culprit tries to acquire the financial information such as Card number, PIN other information required for online transactions or to operate your account. The information is asked over the phone or by creating fake email account in the name of banks or government departments. Never respond to any such request and inform your banker about the same.

The following are some useful tips to safeguard from card frauds:

a. On receipt of the ATM/Debit/Credit card, immediately sign at the back of the card with permanent black ink. This is important as one can prove the ownership of the card in case of requirement.

b. Change Personal Identification Number (PIN) immediately on receipt of the same from the bank to safeguard against any chance of it being noted or copied by anyone during transit.

c. Memorize one's PIN but not write it on the ATM/Debit/Credit card or any other place.

d. Immediately inform the Card issuing bank/agency in case of the card getting lost.

e. Keep a record of all your account numbers and card issuing bank/agency contact details in a secure place so that you can easily access it and report loss or misuse of the card.

f. Always keep the PIN secret. Change it frequently.

g. Neither hand over your card nor disclose your PIN to anybody. Handing over your card and disclosing PIN to someone is like authorizing that person to withdraw money from your Bank account.

h. It is mandatory for all banks in India to send SMS for all ATM/ Debit/Credit card transactions to the registered mobile number of the Cardholder irrespective of the amount of the transaction. One must ensure to register his mobile number with his banker.

i. Check all the alerts on your mobile immediately as and when received and read its contents carefully.

j. One must, as far as possible, use ATM machine of the same bank whose ATM/Debit/Credit card they use.

k. One must find out, before withdrawing money from the ATM, about the number of mandatory free transactions (financial and non-financial), per month, permitted for use of own bank ATM as well as other bank's ATM.

l. One must know the daily cash withdrawal limit.

m. The card holder must know the charges, if any, applicable on the use of an ATM. Card holder can reach out to the bank to understand these charges.

n. Be clear about the need for an International Debit Card. Find out from your bank about the type of your card and ask only for the one required by you.

o. In case of a Credit Card it is advisable to have minimum card limit based on your typical spending pattern.

p. Always verify your Credit Card statements carefully immediately on receipt of the same. You can also track the card activity in case you have online access.

q. Report to the Credit Card issuing bank/agency immediately in case of any doubtful transaction.

r. Inform your card issuing bank/agency immediately in case of change in your address.

s. Carry with you the cards which you use frequently. As far as possible, keep the cards separate from your wallet.

t. Expired cards should be disposed of safely and securely as fraudsters can activate them by loading with fresh user data. Lakhs of rupees have siphoned off by fraudsters using this method. It is very important to destroy the expired cards by cutting the card in to a number of small pieces. Throw away the pieces separately in a way that the same cannot be joined together.

21. Safety and Security tips while using Cards at ATM

About 99% of the cases of ATM frauds happen only because of low alertness. We need to be alert and careful all the time. There are two stages of performing an ATM transactions i.e. pre-processing and processing and post processing. Some tips that can be used as precautionary measures for these situations or stages are shared below:

a. Pre-processing Situations

Pre-processing situations are those where a user can be exposed to possible fraud risks if not analysed carefully before the ATM transaction is initiated or before entering into the ATM booth. The following tips will reduce the possibility of a fraud:

1. As far as possible use your own bank's ATM.
2. Must ensure that the ATM is not located in an isolated location and is in a well-lit area.
3. As far as possible use the ATM which you regularly use.
4. Observe your surroundings, particularly in the night. In case you notice some suspicious person around, do not use the ATM.
5. Must remember your Card PIN before entering the ATM booth.
6. Senior citizens must ensure to use their own bank's ATM. If possible must take another known/reliable person with them. Let someone, at home, know that where you are going and with whom.

7. Have your ATM card out of your purse/pocket and ready to use.
8. Do not use the ATM If the machine displays error message twice consequently. Taking help of other unknown person, in such cases, can be very risky and lead to loss of money. The situation may be created by someone to trap the card user.
9. If one observes that somebody is following him, must immediately inform the Police and go away from that particular ATM.

b. Processing and Post Processing Situation

Processing situations are those that can occur once the cardholder starts operating the ATM whereas post processing situations are those that occur after the completion of the transaction. The following tips will reduce the possibility of a fraud:

1. Be very alert inside the ATM booth in case the ATM is installed in such a closed door set-up.
2. Close the door of the booth from inside.
3. Observe the surroundings to see if any suspicious looking device such as a camera or mirror which does not look like a bank installed equipment has been fixed to record your action to steal your pin or card details. Don't use the ATM in such a scenario.
4. Before inserting your card into the card slot ensure that the card slot is looking normal or not tampered with.
5. The skimmer fixes a skimming devise into the card slot. When the card travels through the same,

the magnetic information on the card such as the name and bank account number embedded in the magnetic strip get recorded. In case you encounter any problem while inserting your card into the card slot or feel that the card entry into the card slot is not smooth CANCEL the transaction by pressing the Cancel button on the ATM keyboard. Change your password by visiting some other ATM immediately.

6. The other way adopted by these fraudsters is that they insert a thin filament underneath the enter button on the ATM keyboard which make the enter button jammed. After inserting the card and typing out the PIN, the cardholder would not be able to continue the operation as the enter button remains stuck and does not work. When the cardholder leaves the ATM, the fraudster enters and removes the sheet and presses the enter button and withdraws the money. In such cases, the cardholder must CANCEL the transaction and inform the bank immediately rather than leaving the ATM thinking that the transaction has been automatically cancelled.

7. Beware of "Shoulder Surfing". Shield your PIN from onlookers by using your body while using walk-up ATMs.

8. Cover the ATM keypad with your hand while entering your PIN and amount.

9. Report immediately if the ATM does not work. Cancel your transaction and report the matter to the bank on the telephone numbers displayed in the ATM booth.

10. Avoid asking the help of strangers.
11. If the card is confiscated by the machine or is lost or stolen, get the card blocked immediately.
12. Always press the 'CANCEL' key before moving away from the ATM.
13. After completing your transaction and before leaving the ATM booth, check that you have your Card and Receipt.
14. Must also ensure that the ATM Screen is in the same mode from when you started the transaction.
15. Avoid counting cash inside or outside the ATM booth. Keep the cash in your pocket.
16. Lock your car doors every time you are in the car post a bank or ATM transaction.

22. Point of Sale (POS) System

It is very important to know about the POS system as we use our Credit and Debit cards to make payment of our purchases of goods and services from various retail and other outlets having POS machines. POS machines are installed at various retail and other commercial outlets to handle transactions relating to cash and credit sales. Transactions with Debit Card are cash sales as the value of goods and services purchased by us are debited to our connected bank account simultaneously. Purchases by using Credit Cards are on short time credit basis, which the cardholder pays as per the arrangement with the Credit Card issuers.

23. Process of use of debit/credit card for retail transactions at Point of sale terminal

Step 1: The merchant swipes or dips debit/credit card at point of sale terminal.

Step 2: The merchant enters the transaction amount in the POS machine.

Step 3: The POS machine prompts for the entry of card PIN.

Step 4: The cardholder enters the PIN. The transaction is confirmed immediately once the cardholder enters the correct PIN in the machine. The transaction amount is debited to the bank account of the cardholder simultaneously.

Step 5: Debit/Credit card handed over back to the cardholder by the merchant.

24. Safety Tips-Uses of Debit/Credit Cards at Merchant Establishments

a. Always enter the PIN yourself.
b. Cover the keyboard with your hand while entering your PIN.
c. Enter the PIN when screen asks for it.
d. Always check the transaction amount before entering your PIN.
e. Collect your card back and merchant receipt after the completion of your transaction.

f. Must verify carefully that the card given back to you by the merchant is your card only.

g. Always check that alert for the transaction has been received on your mobile.

h. Must read the alert message on your mobile to see that the amount of the transaction is correct.

i. Never ask the assistance of the merchants to record your PIN.

j. Never share your PIN with anyone.

k. Never write the PIN on the card or keep the written copy of PIN with the card.

l. Never voice out your PIN to the cashier of the merchant.

m. Never allow the cashier or merchant to take your card out of your sight to make sure that they are not copying or **skimming** your card detail.

n. Never allow anyone to take a photocopy of your card.

25. Victim of Card frauds-Some case studies

The case studies of card frauds given below are actual instances, either reported in the newspapers or reported to the author by the victims themselves. A careful study of these cases can help one to understand how innocent card users are cheated:

Case No. 1: A case of Card Skimming:

One of the victims of ATM fraud, living in Hyderabad, narrated that when he got up in the morning he checked his mobile and found a few alert messages. These messages were from his bank about the debit of ₹40,000/- from his account towards ATM withdrawals using his debit card in one of the ATM terminal in Bengaluru. He checked his card and was surprised to see that the original card was with him. He immediately contacted the Bank thinking that the same may be an error on the bank's part and could not think about the fraudulent withdrawal of his hard-earned money by any fraudster. He kept this money in his account for the payment of examination fees. He approached the bank branch and inquired about these debits. Bank confirmed about the withdrawal toward use of his ATM card. He requested them to reverse the debit entries as he has not used the card for the same. The victim told and proved them that the original card was in his possession. He informed the bank that he never shared his card or PIN with anybody. The victim also informed the bank that last time when he used the card in an ATM booth, located in a lonely place, where he felt that everything was not in order and possibly his card information was stolen through skimming.

The bank refused to refund the amount. The victim got relief when he approached Banking Ombudsman on the advice of the author of this book.

In view of the above we need to learn that:

- ◄ Never use ATM booths located in lonely places.
- ◄ Must be alert and ensure that no skimming devise has been placed near the ATM.

Case No. 2: Victim left the ATM booth without cancelling the incomplete transaction:

A woman was allegedly cheated when she took the help of an unidentified person when she failed to get cash while using her card. She made a number of failed attempts to withdraw money and left the ATM booth when an unknown man told her that ATM is not working and she should try some other ATM. After about an hour, the victim received an alert message from her bank about debit of ₹15000/- from her account. The woman called up her bank and enquired about the transaction. The victim said that she left the ATM booth without cancelling the transaction as she was not aware that she was supposed to cancel the transaction as she had faced this issue for the first time.

Important Points to note:

- ◄ Must cancel by pressing cancel button on the keypad in case cash is not dispensed. Must remember to press the cancel not only for the incomplete transactions but also after completing the transaction.
- ◄ Inform the bank over phone about such situations before leaving the ATM booth.

Case No.3: Taking help of unknown person inside the ATM booth is very risky:

A Senior Citizen was cheated of ₹60000/- at an unmanned ATM booth. He reported that he visited an ATM booth to withdraw ₹10000/-. When he was having a problem in operating the ATM a man offered him help. The accused helped him and gave him ₹10000/- and his ATM card. When the victim reached home, he found that the ATM card was of another bank. He thought that it was a mistake but soon received a message on his mobile that ₹30000/- has been withdrawn from his bank account and ₹30000/- has been transferred to other account.

One must learn the following from the above incident:

◄ Never take help of unknown persons.

◄ Never hand over the Card to anybody.

◄ Never disclose PIN to anybody.

Case No. 4: Card Cloning:

A number of individuals have been duped of their hard-earned money by international fraudsters operating from overseas. In most of the cases the money has been siphoned off from the salary accounts of the individual through mystery purchases and withdrawals from an overseas location.

The victim reported that they suspect that fraudsters had possibly cloned the debit cards and also had access to the PIN that is required to complete the transaction.

One must learn the following to avoid such type of frauds:

◄ On receipt of Card and PIN one must change the PIN immediately.

◄ One must change the PIN at a regular intervals.

◄ One should only opt the cards for domestic use. Get the card enabled for international usages only if required.

◄ Check with your banker and get your card disabled for international usages if the same is issued both for domestically and internationally usages.

Case No. 5: Card stolen and misused:

ATM/Debit card of a woman was stolen from her purse when she was at a cafe. She came to know about the theft immediately when she checked her purse for making payment of the bill. However, she didn't discuss with anybody and even did not inform her bank. The next day she received alert messages from the bank on her mobile about the withdrawal of ₹50000/-.

In view of the above we must note the following point:

◄ One must take care of his/her card and keep the same at a safe place and well protected in a purse or bag.

◄ One must get the card hot listed immediately in case the same is lost or not traceable by calling the banks helpline.

◄ One must maintain the secrecy of the PIN at all the time.

Case No. 6: Disclosing your card detail over phone is very risky:

The victim of an ATM/Debit card fraud informed that he got a call from an unknown person claiming that he is a bank officer and told him that his Card had been blocked. He asked him to provide his card number and the three-digit CVV number. The victim gave all details. The victim got another call from the same person and he asked him to read out the one time password (OTP) received on his mobile which he provided without thinking about the consequences. After a few minutes when he received another message of debit of ₹22000/- toward one online transaction he realized about his mistake.

One should learn the following from the above incident:

- Calls from unknown and unconfirmed persons asking about one's bank account, cards, CVV number, PIN, OTP or any other personal information should not be entertained.
- Must bring this to the notice of your bank about all such calls.

Case No. 7: Giving card to friend/relative for operating ATM is very risky:

The victim, a working woman, gave her card to one of her friends to withdraw the money from the ATM. She also told her the PIN. Her friend withdrew the money from an ATM and handed over the same to the victim along with the card. The mobile number of the victim's father was registered in her account. After 5 days of withdrawal of the money from an ATM, while checking mobile of her father, she was surprised to see an alert message about the debit of ₹47000/- from her account. On inquiry from her friend, she told that she took the help of two unknown persons who offered help when two transactions failed while operating the ATM.

The following are some of the important points to learn from the above incident:

- ◄ Never handover your card to anybody even to your friends. The friend may not be very confident as to how to withdraw money from ATM.
- ◄ Must ensure that the mobile number of the person who is operating the card is registered with the bank.

Case No. 8: It is very risk to disclose your financial information in response to unknown e-mails:

The victim, a government servant, provided all his financial information, personal information and debit card number and PIN number in response to an e-mail, purporting to be from Income Tax Department regarding the refund of the income tax already paid by the victim. On the basis of the information provided by the victim the gang of criminals cloned his debit card and made a number of purchases from different merchant locations up to the balance available in the victim's account. When the victim received alert messages he got his card hot listed, but by that time all the money was used up.

The following are very important points to learn:

- ◄ Banks/Income Tax Department or any other financial agency never asks for PIN number, Password or similar access information for credit card/debit card or bank account etc. through e-mail.
- ◄ One should never respond to such e-mails and not to share information relating to their Cards or bank accounts.

Section 3

MANAGEMENT OF BANK FRAUDS-CHEQUE AND CARD

1. Management of Bank Frauds

As a customer of a bank, it is important to know about the remedies available in case of any fraudulent transaction in our bank account.

Reserve Bank of India and all other banks have taken a number of initiatives to check all types of bank frauds, but we still find incidents of bank frauds being reported almost every day in print or electronic media.

Customers on their part want to get back the amount debited to their accounts, without their consent, immediately, but the banks at times do not restore the funds promptly making the customer suffer.

The directions of Reserve bank of India, as given below, in respect of compensating the customer are very clear and part of the customer service directives issued to the banks:

1. In case of any fraud, if the bank branch is convinced that an irregularity/fraud has been committed by its staff towards any constituent, the branch should at once acknowledge its liability and pay the just claim.

2. In cases where banks are at fault, they should compensate the customer without demur.
3. In cases where neither the bank nor the customer are at fault and the issue lies elsewhere in the system, then also the bank should compensate the customer (up to a limit) as per the approved compensation policy of the respective banks.

In this section of the book, the author has focused on immediate and possible solutions available to the bank customer in case one becomes a victim of bank fraud. It is necessary for the victim to understand, what to do in case of fraudulent transaction in his/her account and how to justify the same to the bank and other forums about his/her claim.

The detailed guidelines are given below to help victims in respect of cheques and card frauds:

2. What to do in case of Cheque Frauds

In section 1 of the book, we explained the use of cheques and type of cheque frauds. The precaution to safeguard our self from cheque frauds are also covered.

In case one becomes a victim of cheque fraud, some key steps to claim their hard-earned money are suggested below:

a. **Inform the bank expeditiously**, in writing, about the unauthorized debit in your account.
b. Request the bank to arrange and **provide** you the **original cheque**.

c. Request the bank to note **stop payment** of all other unissued cheques to avoid any further chances of cheque fraud.

d. Examine the forged cheque carefully to find out the **type of cheque fraud** (Counterfeit/Altered/Stolen Cheque) or to observe any defect in the cheque, which the banker has not observed before passing the same.

e. Please lodge your complaint with the bank as suggested below for different type of cheque frauds:

Type of cheque fraud	Observations	Suggestions
Counterfeit/Altered cheque	1. Where is the original cheque? 2. To whom the original Cheque was issued? 3. In case of a cash cheque paid on the counter of the bank, ask the bank to provide the CCTV footage of the transaction-taking place. 4. In case paid in clearing to some other bank. Ask for the full detail of the payee.	1. The bank needs to refund the amount immediately if a counterfeit cheque is paid. The bank should be fully equipped to recognize a counterfeit cheque. So write to the bank to refund the money. Also, claim up to date interest.

contd.

		2. In case the bank provides you all the details as asked by looking at the paid cheque, please give your feedback to the bank to enable them to catch the culprit.
Stolen Cheque	1. Find out how the cheque was stolen and written.

2. Signature and other detail on the cheque.

3. In case of a cash cheque paid on the counter of the bank ask the bank to provide the CCTV footage of the transaction-taking place.

4. In case paid in clearing to some other bank. Ask for the full detail of the payee to find out whether paid into a fictitious account opened by the fraudsters in the same name in which the cheque was issued or otherwise. | If one observes any discrepancies, highlight the same to the bank and ask them to compensate. |

3. What to do in case of other type of Cheque Frauds

In respect of the following other type of Cheque frauds in which the account of the victim is not involved but cheated by the fraudsters using one or the other trick:

a. Issuing cheques drawn on closed accounts for some consideration.

b. Cheque drawn as to look like demand draft or banker cheques issued in favour of the victims toward one or the other consideration.

In these cases, the involvement of banks is only to the extent that they can provide the information of the account holder whose cheques are used. The account holders involvement can be proved only with proper investigation. In such cases, the complaint should not only to be made to the bank but also to the Police immediately.

4. What to do in case of Card (ATM/Debit/Credit Card) Frauds

We have already learned about different types of frauds relating to card transactions. These frauds are only possible when the fraudster acquires or steals our card or card details as well as our Personal Identification Number (PIN). We can prevent or at least reduce chances of card frauds if we follow the tips as suggested in this book.

The victims of card frauds need to take the following steps, for different type of card frauds, to recover their hard-earned money:

a. Card switched with Fake Card (Card Stolen)

Check your card on receipt of the alert message from your bank on your mobile in respect of any fraudulent withdrawal of money from an ATM. If you notice you are in possession of a fake card exchanged with your original card by the fraudster, whose help you may have sought while operating the ATM, immediately take the following steps:

- **Contact the card-issuing bank** and get your card blocked.
- Request the bank to immediately arrange the **CCTV footage** of that particular transaction.
- **File written complaint** with the Bank narrating the full details of the incident.
- Request the bank to take appropriate action for recovery of the amount.
- Lodge complaint with the Police and provide them the CCTV footage showing the picture of the culprit.

b. ATM card with the cardholder but money withdrawn from an ATM

A number of cases of ATM fraud came to light where the original card was in the possession of the cardholder but the account was debited toward ATM transactions. Use of cards, in similar manner, at POS locations toward purchase of goods are also common. The cardholders i.e. the victims in most of the cases noticed the debit of their account when they received alert messages from banks.

The above types of frauds are the work of criminal gangs whose members are spread around a number of cities having strong network. They collect full details of cards and PIN of the cardholders using different tricks and immediately pass on the information to other cities or countries where they clone the card and then misuse them.

In such cases, the victim on receiving the alert message must take the following steps:

- Visit the nearest ATM booth, use your card, and print out your statement of account to prove your place of presence. These steps will also prove that the original card is in your possession and the card used elsewhere was a cloned one.
- Contact the bank help desk and get the card hot listed.
- Visit the nearest police station and lodge a complaint, mentioning the full details. Show, the original card to the Police officer and take their acknowledgement of having seen the card in your possession.
- Lodge a written complaint with the bank, provide them full details and show them the card in your possession. Request the bank to investigate without loss of time, provide full detail and CCTV footage of the transaction.
- Request the bank to compensate the loss.

If the matter is not resolved within a month from the date of your complaint or not settled to your satisfaction, approach Banking Ombudsman under whose jurisdiction the branch against whom the complaint was made is situated. The important features of the Banking Ombudsman Scheme are provided in the subsequent paragraphs.

The victim also has the option to lodge a police complaint giving full details of the fraudulent transaction.

5. Other forum for immediate relief for Bank Customers

It is very important to know about the following, other forums available to bank customers in case they are not satisfied with their banker on the outcome of the redressal of their grievances:

a. Banking Ombudsman Scheme

Banking Ombudsman Scheme was introduced by Reserve Bank of India and made effective with effect from the year 1995. The scheme was reviewed in the year 2002 and further in the year 2006. The main objective of the scheme is speedy resolution of complaints relating to certain services rendered by banks. All Schedule Commercial Banks, Regional Rural Banks and Schedule Primary Co-operative Banks are covered under the scheme. Over the past three years, Ombudsman handled 245673 complaints and disposed of 233109 complaints.

The following are some of the important features of the scheme:

- Any person, having any complaint against a Bank relating to the deficiency in banking or other services, can file a complaint to the Banking Ombudsman. The number of such services has been mentioned in the scheme. The list covers most banking services which a customer or any other person is entitled to receive from banks while dealing with them.

- Complaints can be filed against any deficiency one observes or faces which are against the directive and instructions of Reserve Bank of India.

- One can file a complaint against any type of unauthorized debit/fraudulent transaction in their bank account.

- Complaint to Banking Ombudsman can be made in writing duly signed as well as online. One can lodge the complaint at the office of the Banking Ombudsman under whose jurisdiction the bank branch of the complainant is situated. At present about 15 Banking Ombudsman have been appointed by the Reserve Bank of India and their offices are located mostly in state capitals.

- The complaint can be filed with Banking Ombudsman only after the representation or complaint made to the respective bank by the complainant is not replied to within a period of one month from the bank receiving the representation or complaint or if the complainant is not satisfied with the reply given by the bank.

- The complaint to Banking Ombudsman is to be made within one year from the date of receipt of the reply from the bank. If no reply is received, the complaint can be filed within one year and one month from the date of the representation or complaint to the bank.
- The complaint to the Banking Ombudsman can be filed through a complainant's authorized representative but not through an advocate.
- The Banking Ombudsman in respect of complaints filed by the complaints charges no fee.

If one is not satisfied with the resolution or the decision of the Banking Ombudsman, one can approach the appellate authority. The appellate Authority is vested with Deputy Governor, Reserve Bank of India. Appeal can be filed within 30 days of the date of receipt of the award from the Banking Ombudsman as per the Banking Ombudsman Scheme.

In case the complainant is still not satisfied with the outcome of his complaint, there is an option to approach the Consumer forum.

b. Consumer Forum

The option of approaching consumer forum is always open to us for our grievances against any matter relating to the services offered by the banks under the consumer protection act. A numbers of victims of bank frauds have received relief from the consumer forum.

Important information for filing the complaint with consumer forum is furnished below:

a. Complainant can file the complaint himself or through an authorized person.

b. Complaint can be filed as per the value of good or service as mentioned below:

Jurisdiction	Value of goods or service
District forum	Not to exceed ₹20 lakhs
State Commission	Above ₹20 lakhs but not exceeding ₹ One crore
National Commission	Above ₹ One Crore

c. The complaint can be filed at the place where the opposite party resides or carries out business or personally works for gain and/or where the cause of action wholly or partly arose.

d. Time limit for filling the complaint to the forum or commission has been prescribed as "within two years" from the date on which the cause of action arises. The complaint can be taken up even after two years provided the complainant is able to satisfy the forum or the commission about the cause of the delay.

e. Appeals against the order of the district forum to the state commission to the national commission are to be filled within the prescribed period of 30 days. However the appeal can be entertained beyond 30 days on sufficient grounds to justify the delay.

6. Fraud Cases Settled by Banking Ombudsman

Banking Ombudsman in their annual reports furnishes detail of exemplary cases dealt with by them. These cases are in respect of complaints of bank customers on various issues pertaining to customer service. The reports have also highlighted number of cheque frauds and ATM/Debit/Credit Cards frauds apart from other type of bank frauds dealt with by the Banking Ombudsman.

Some of the fraud cases dealt with by Banking Ombudsman (BO) are furnished hereunder:

a. Cheque Fraud Cases

Case No. 1: Cheque Stolen from banks drop-box and encashed with material alteration:

The complainant had issued a multi-city Cheque favouring his supplier. The cheque was deposited in the drop-box for the credit of his account. The drop-box was broken open and its contents were stolen. The instrument in question being one among the stolen ones, was subjected to fraudulent alteration and was presented through clearing. It's proceeds was credited to the account of a fraudster with another bank.

In the above case, the Banking Ombudsman (BO) observed deficiencies on the part of all the three banks involved. While presenting bank had failed to provide adequate security to its drop box the collecting bank had not scrupulously complied with the Know Your Customer (KYC) guidelines with respect to the account maintained in the name of the fraudster who encashed the instrument. The payee bank had overlooked the material alterations. The BO, therefore, ordered all the three banks to share the loss in equal proportions and make good the amount to the complainant.

Case No. 2: A case where neither the bank nor the customer is at Fault:

The complainant had deposited a cheque for collection in the cheque drop box of his bank provided in the ATM kiosk. However, the cheque amount was not credited to his account. The bank official informed that the cheque was stolen by miscreants from the drop box and misused. FIR about the theft was lodged with the Police. As per extant RBI guidelines, in such cases where there is no fault of bank and the customer, the onus of payment of compensation (up to a limit) lies with the collecting bank as part of the Board approved policy. Banking Ombudsman (BO) advised the bank to pay the cheque amount with interest at saving bank rate for delayed period.

Case No. 3: A case of Forged Cheque:

Complainant alleged that an amount of ₹270000/- was withdrawn from her account through forged cheque while the original cheque was with the complainant. On taking up the matter, the concerned bank mentioned that on receiving the complaint, they immediately contacted the collecting banker and froze the balance amount of ₹219961.82 of the account in which the amount in question was credited. The account holder, who received credit in his account, was not found at the recorded address. In the conciliation meeting both banks claimed that they had taken adequate care while presenting/passing the cheque and there was no lapse on their side. However, as regards the collecting bank, it was observed that they had not followed KYC norms properly while opening the account of the person who committed fraud and in whose account the amount was credited. As regard the presenting bank, as there was apparent difference in the signature of the complainant, on the cheque and specimen signature recorded with the bank, the bank should have made some enquiry/verification before paying the cheque of such a big amount. Besides, the quality of paper of the forged cheque should have raised some doubt. Both the banks were found negligent in discharging their duties. In view of the above, an Award was passed directing both the banks to pay ₹25000/- each and credit the account of the complainant with ₹270000/- by which it was fraudulently debited along with interest at SB rate.

b. Card fraud cases

Case No. 1: Card data stolen by placing skimming devise:

A complainant alleged that although she had not visited the ATM, ₹80000/- had been withdrawn from her account. The CCTV footage showed someone else withdrawing the amount. The complainant had received the SMS alert. but the disputed transaction happened at 23.53 hours and 00.05 hours when she was asleep. According to her she had last gone to the ATM terminal a month back.

The records indicated that the complainant's version was true and the time of transaction raised more suspicion around a fraud actually having taken place. During the discussion with bank, it became known that in that particular ATM machine, a fraudster had placed a skimming devise and had copied details. An FIR had been lodged with the Police. The Banking Ombudsman (BO) contended that it was not the complainant's fault that the magnetic data of her card had been copied and used later to her detriment. The complainant sought repayment of the disputed amount. The bank agreed and paid the amount with value date.

Case No. 2: No alert message for usage of card received by the victim on the registered mobile:

The complainant's debit card was used resulting in his account being debited by ₹4.82 lakh for POS transaction made in two tranches. A written complaint was immediately lodged with the branch at the first instance to block the card, however, his account was again debited for another transaction for ATM withdrawal. The complainant requested for reversal of the total disputed amounts together with interest at 21%.

The bank initially stated that without compromise of PIN details, the transactions could not have happened which meant that the complainant had compromised the PIN. Further, the bank disputed the request for blocking the card given by the complainant. While perusing the documents submitted, it was observed that bank had not sent any SMS alert to the registered mobile number, which was very important evidence in this case, since the disputed transaction had happened over a period. Had the bank sent SMS alerts, it would have alerted the complainant and further fraudulent transactions in the account could have been avoided. The complainant challenged this by saying that he was receiving regular promotional alerts from the bank and was ready to produce the same to prove that his mobile number was registered with the bank. The complainant also produced a copy of the letter given to the bank requesting for blocking of the card, which the bank failed to act upon. Since all the bank's contentions were not appropriate and incorrect, the bank was advised by Banking Ombudsman (BO) to reimburse the complainant the entire disputed amount together with interest at saving bank rate.

Case No. 3: Never take help of strangers:

An eighty-year-old man complained that his account was debited with ₹10000/-, though he had not received cash, he received the SMS instantaneously. A perusal of the footage indicated that the complainant had handed over the ATM card to another person who was standing with him in the ATM booth. The individual told the complainant that the machine was not functioning properly and when the complainant left, the stranger pocketed the money himself. An FIR was lodged and the culprit was nabbed. Although Banking Ombudsman (BO) rejected the complaint, because the complainant had divulged confidential information. The alacrity of the Banking Ombudsman (BO), the concerned bank and police officials helped the complainant to get back his money.

7. Conclusion

It is observed that bank frauds are growing and one of the common factor in all the fraud cases is that victims take things very easy and are careless while handling financial transactions. It is necessary to adhere to all safe banking tips provided from time to time by the Banks, RBI and other consumer forums. Therefore, there is always a need for us to be alert and careful while handling our financial transactions.

In case of Cheque transactions, it is important for us to do the same very carefully as mentioned above, but at the same time, the bank staff that is passing our cheques for payment must not only be alert and careful but also have an analytical approach while examining any cheque or document. They must be trained to recognize fraudulent instruments and always be one-step ahead of these fraudsters to protect the interest of their customers.

In case of card frauds, it is observed by the author that the same are happening due to not only the cardholder's carelessness, but also one or the other factor relating to the deficiency in providing a completely secure environment to the cardholders. It is therefore necessary for banks to think about all the security aspects to make the card transactions fool proof.

Bank customers awareness about options available to them in cases of fraudulent transactions in their bank accounts is also lacking. In case of any cheating or fraud, customers must immediately take up the matter with their banks and other agencies as suggested in this book.

Banks must have a sympathetic attitude toward fraud victims. They should also must arrange awareness workshops and educational programs from time to time on prevention of frauds for the benefit of their customers.

In respect of fraud cases, the coordination between the bank branches and the local police is very important to nab culprits. There is an urgent need to have a coordination committee of bank branch staff and local police personnel with proper action plans in place to handle and solve fraud cases more efficiently.

Banks must provide practical training to all senior citizens about the use of ATM/Debit card before issuing the same to them. As it is evident that most of the victims of the ATM frauds are senior citizen and they are at risk due to lack of knowledge.

The author would also like to request and advise all its readers to use ATM and other services of the bank only once they are fully confident to use the same. If you need help talk to your banker not strangers.

Fraudsters are becoming clever and more tech savvy by the day. While this book covers some broad aspects around this subject, I do hope that the little information and knowledge I have shared with readers will benefit them and help prevent being cheated while making financial transactions. I would like to end my book with the following quote by Bruce Barton:

"Sometime when I consider what tremendous consequences come from little things…I am tempted to think…there are no little things."

www.ingramcontent.com/pod-product-compliance
Lightning Source LLC
Chambersburg PA
CBHW020436220526
45464CB00002B/728